Endorsements

This memory journal is the perfect gift for busy moms longing to leave a "legacy-mark of love" etched into their child's heart! Only seconds of your time will invest rich and real dividends to be treasured for all of time.
Nancy Gardner
Life Coach, **Author of "*Authentically Alive*",** and Lover of Jesus, www.risenwings.com, Castle Rock, CO

I am sure as you re-use this perpetual memory journal year after year, you will see as I did, that it will help foster a wonderful relationship between you and your children. Sherri's encouragement, example, grace and practical application ideas have been extremely beneficial as we raised our four children!
Tish Dray
Athletic trainer, mother of 4 - ages 24, 22, 20, 16 - Lancaster, MA

Sherri has a zealous heart for using her gifts for God's purposes. She has a refreshing, vibrant way of expressing the joys and the challenges of motherhood, while inspiring mothers of all ages.
Soozie Schneider
Faculty Initiatives Director, **Rivendell Institute at Yale,** Hamden, CT

In *"Mom's Moments - Smiles to Remember"*, Sherri skillfully combines the wisdom found in scripture with her thoughtfully written poems. It has been a source of encouragement and an indispensable tool in keeping track of those special moments that happen most every day.
Rebecca King
Adoption Social Worker & Mother of 3 – 10, 8, 5 - Highlands Ranch, CO

Sherri's poems gently teach timeless truths in this delightful approach to a 'mama journal' and devotional that is easy to use.
Sharon Gamble
Author of: *Sweet Selah Moments: Encouragement for Everyday Living,* www.sweetselah.org, Dover, NH

I deeply appreciate Sherri's commitment to the care and development of young moms and their children. Childrearing is an art form and Sherri's poetry adds a perfect touch of the day-to-day as well as the timeless Word of God.
Kathryn Roy
Executive Director, **Love INC - Love In the Name of Christ,**
www.loveinclittleton.org, Littleton, CO

As a working mom time is precious, but so are those once-in-a-lifetime experiences with my children. *"Mom's Moments - Smiles to Remember"* teaches me positive parenting tools in an entertaining and thoughtful way and has a place for me to write down my own memories before they are consumed by the busyness of the day!
Kathy Steinhaus French
Genetic Counselor & Mother of two, Santa Ana, CA

Sherri's engaging and creative keepsake memory journal and daily devotional will provide daily sustenance and practical godly advice, along with some much-needed smiles to lighten the road for that devoted and dedicated mom in your life. And she'll have the opportunity to journal her children's "firsts" and create a keepsake worth remembering and cherishing!
Linda Moore
Founder & Director of **by design ministries,**
www.bydesignministries.org, Carlisle, MA

In this day filled with screen time distractions, Sherri brings sweet encouragement and some fun new ideas to mothers of all ages to refocus their eyes on Christ in order to obtain the wisdom, power and love to become the moms He wants each to be. This will become a treasure you'll return to often through the years as you record your precious memories.
Rev. Dr. Samuel & Esther Hollo
Pastor and Director of **The Carpenter's Workshop,**
A Biblical, comprehensive, preventive, parenting curriculum
www.carpenters-workshop.org, Alton Bay, NH

MOM'S MOMENTS

Smiles to Remember

Keepsake Memory Journal
Daily Devotional

366 Inspirational, Heart-Warming, & Humorous Poems
366 Daily Bible Verses

Sherri Martinelli

XULON PRESS

Xulon Press
2301 Lucien Way #415
Maitland, FL 32751
407.339.4217
www.xulonpress.com

Printed in the United States of America.

ISBN-13: 978-1-54566-249-6

To: Nichole

From: Sherri Martinelli

Date: March 5, 2022

Occasion: Meeting you today at Casa del Herrero

It was a delight to meet you today when my long-time friend, Jane Defnet, gave my sister & I a tour.

With two little ones and "running" Casa del Herrero, I thought you could use some encouragement & smiles. Hope you find lots of inspiration, new ideas & smiles in this keepsake journal as you record milestones, special moments, kid quotes & more in this journal.

Blessings to you, Sherri

MOM'S MOMENTS ~ *Smiles to Remember*
Background Story and Instructions

Over 25 years ago, the perpetual calendar, *Mother's Moments,* was born. Through the years, these heartwarming illustrations and original poems brought joy, inspiration, and encouragement to mothers and moms-to-be world-wide with over 100,000 copies sold!

The author, Sherri Martinelli, used her calendar as a Memory Journal, recording all the first-time milestones, memories or special moments of her three children. Today, as a motivational speaker, she sees that parents are still craving guidance, new ideas, wisdom, encouragement, and humor as they take on the often overwhelming, yet God-given opportunity to parent their precious gifts from God, their children.

Now redesigned, **Mom's Moments ~ Smiles to Remember,** is a *Keepsake Memory Journal and Daily Devotional.* Each original poem is supported by a corresponding Bible verse, which is cross-referenced in the *Bible Index* at the end of this book. This journal will give you daily inspiration with a quick and easy way of recording, in just a couple of words, all those special moments for your children or grandchildren, on the specific day and year they happened. Periodically, when there is more to share, use the extra lines provided at the end of the book. The memory can be recorded on the original date with a reference to the specific page at the end of the book where the memory continues.

This is a perpetual journal that can last a lifetime for all your children.

Examples how to use **Mom's Moments~ Smiles to Remember** *Journal*

March 5		More – See Page
2019	Scott is born! 8lbs. 3 oz.!! 21 in. long	**375**
2022	1st family beach vacation!	
2023	Baby Danielle was Cambria's "Show & Tell" – 1st Grade	
2028	Scott fell off his bike, broke arm, helmet saved his life!	
2029	Danielle sang a song she made up for Scott's birthday.	
2032	Cambria gets Driver's License! Yikes!!	

*Enjoy and treasure each moment with your
child and see God's faithfulness year after year!*

January 1

Wake up! Enjoy today!
God made it perfect in every way.
So, find the good! Avoid the bad!
Teach your child to rejoice and be glad.

More – See Page

20____ _____ _____

20____ _____ _____

20____ _____ _____

20____ _____ _____

20____ _____ _____

20____ _____ _____

Rejoice in the Lord always.
I will again say it again: Rejoice!
Philippians 4:4

January 2

I look around my house, and it's only clutter that I can see.
How much is really that important to my husband, our children and me?
Do we really need it? Would we miss it?
And does it bring us smiles and joy?
Does it hold memories? Is it worth keeping?
Or just outgrown clothes or toy?
So many others have so little, our clutter just collects the dust.
Help me sort, give away, and only keeping special memories or a *must*.

More – See Page

20___ _____ _____

20___ _____ _____

20___ _____ _____

20___ _____ _____

20___ _____ _____

20___ _____ _____

"Don't store up treasures here on earth,
were moths eat them and rust destroys them,
and were thieves break in and steal
Store your treasures in heaven, where moths and rust
cannot destroy, and thieves do not break in and steal.
Wherever your treasure is,
there the desires of your heart will also be."
Matthew 6:19-21

January 3

"Please do forgive me!"
That can leave you vulnerable, that's true.
But said to your child
Opens a relationship that's new.

More – See Page

20___ _____ _____
_____

20___ _____ _____
_____

20___ _____ _____
_____

20___ _____ _____
_____

20___ _____ _____
_____

20___ _____ _____
_____

Instead be kind to each other,
tenderhearted, forgiving one another,
just as God through Christ has forgiven you.
Ephesians 4:32 NLT

January 4

Did you know some bears
Give birth while in hibernation?
When the mother bear awakens,
Her cubs are already walking, playing and eating.
Though your child's first years
May seem unbearable at times,
Don't be barely there and lose your bearings.
Think of the joy the sleeping bear has missed.
Wake up and enjoy your barefoot beauties.

More – See Page

20____ _____ _____

_____

20____ _____ _____

_____

20____ _____ _____

_____

20____ _____ _____

_____

20____ _____ _____

_____

20____ _____ _____

_____

I'm thanking you, God, from a full heart,
I'm writing the book on your wonders.
I'm whistling, laughing, and jumping for joy;
I'm singing your song, High God.
Psalm 9:1,2 MSG

January 5

Laundry, one of those many household chores
That must be done, but is sort of a bore.
It's a skill each of my children should know
Before they leave home and walk out our door.
But what baffles me the most,
No matter who does the laundry each week,
There is something I can't find
And continually seek.
Two socks per person are worn each day
But after the wash, one's run away!

More – See Page

20___ _____ _____
_____

20___ _____ _____
_____

20___ _____ _____
_____

20___ _____ _____
_____

20___ _____ _____
_____

20___ _____ _____
_____

All who seek the Lord will praise Him.
Their hearts will rejoice with everlasting joy.
Psalms 22:26b

January 6

Lord, am I modeling compassion today
To my children and their friends who come our way?
Do I show them kindness and patience in all I say and do?
Please, help me be an example, so they can see in me. . .YOU!

More – See Page

20____ _____ _____

20____ _____ _____

20____ _____ _____

20____ _____ _____

20____ _____ _____

20____ _____ _____

Therefore, as God's chosen people,
holy and dearly loved,
clothe yourselves with compassion,
kindness, humility, gentleness and patience.
Colossians 3:12

January 7

I wish you could talk and tell me how
To give you comfort from crying now.
I fed you, hugged you, and know you're dry.
Are you too hot? Too cold? Please don't cry.
What should I do? Should I sing you a song?
I pray you will sleep before too long.
Ah. . . you are asleep, how peaceful you look.
I should put you down, I have dinner to cook.
But nothing else matters when I see you rest,
'Cause now is one of the times I love the best.

More – See Page

20___ _____ _____

_____

20___ _____ _____

_____

20___ _____ _____

_____

20___ _____ _____

_____

20___ _____ _____

_____

20___ _____ _____

_____

Then they cried out to the LORD in their trouble,
and he brought them out of their distress.
He stilled the storm to a whisper;
the waves of the sea were hushed.
They were glad when it grew calm.
Psalm 107:28,29,30a

January 8

A child's crisis is very real to him.
Listen to his heart as well as his words.
Don't turn his mountain into a molehill.
When you listen and understand from his level,
He will walk down his mountain to safe ground.

More – See Page

20___ _____ _____

_____

20___ _____ _____

_____

20___ _____ _____

_____

20___ _____ _____

_____

20___ _____ _____

_____

20___ _____ _____

_____

And whatever you do or say,
do it as a representative of the Lord Jesus,
giving thanks through him to God the Father.
Colossians 3:17 NLT

January 9

We call our three-year-old our little CEO.
She is smart, strong-willed and wants everything *just so*!
We've heard it is good to give her options so she can choose,
But we're exhausted, and in battles, we often lose.
It's obvious something has to change,
We need to regain control, and philosophies rearranged.
Lord, please help us! Show us Your plan and heart.
We're tired and frazzled, ready for a new start.

More – See Page

20___ _____ _____

_____

20___ _____ _____

_____

20___ _____ _____

_____

20___ _____ _____

_____

20___ _____ _____

_____

20___ _____ _____

_____

Children, do what your parents tell you.
This is only right.
"Honor your father and mother"
is the first commandment that has a promise
attached to it, namely "so you will live well and have a long life."
Ephesians 6:1-3 MSG

January 10

Dependable, fun, trustworthy, too,
Loving, kind, and plays peek-a-boo.
Not too old and not too young; it's hard to find
The perfect babysitter you have in mind.

More – See Page

20____ _____ _____

20____ _____ _____

20____ _____ _____

20____ _____ _____

20____ _____ _____

20____ _____ _____

And my God will meet all our needs
according to the riches of his glory in Christ Jesus.
Philippians 4:19

January 11

Often God's biggest gifts to us
Come in the littlest of packages. . .our children.

More – See Page

20___ _____ _____

_____

20___ _____ _____

_____

20___ _____ _____

_____

20___ _____ _____

_____

20___ _____ _____

_____

20___ _____ _____

_____

Every good and perfect gift is from above,
coming down from the Father of the heavenly lights,
who does not change like shifting shadows.
James 1:17

January 12

My husband and I need to go out on a date!
But by the time the kids are in bed, it's always too late.
We would like to go to dinner and a good show.
Yet, the cost of a sitter doesn't allow us to go.
What if I traded with our friends down the street?
We like how they *parent,* and their kids are so sweet.
They're the same age as ours and play together so well.
In fact, our youngest gets excited, she comes out of her shell.
Why haven't I thought of this idea before?
We'd get two weekend date nights, out of four!
Just knowing twice a month, we would have time for us two,
It would get me through work, kid's schedules, and all else I do!

More – See Page

20____ _____ _____

20____ _____ _____

20____ _____ _____

20____ _____ _____

20____ _____ _____

20____ _____ _____

As the Scriptures say, "A man leaves his father and mother
and is joined to his wife, and the two are united into one."
Ephesians 5: 31 NLT

January 13

I look in the mirror and what do I see,
But those little wrinkles creeping up on me!
They would appear if I was a mom or not,
But hopefully from laughter and merry thoughts.

More – See Page

20____ _____ _____

20____ _____ _____

20____ _____ _____

20____ _____ _____

20____ _____ _____

20____ _____ _____

Charm is deceptive,
and beauty does not last;
but a woman who fears the Lord
will be greatly praised.
Proverbs 31:30 NLT

January 14

Often when a child asks for something more,
He wants you to say "NO" and close the door.
He knows what's right. What you say is best.
Do not spoil him, this is only a test.

More – See Page

20____ _____ _____

_____

20____ _____ _____

_____

20____ _____ _____

_____

20____ _____ _____

_____

20____ _____ _____

_____

20____ _____ _____

_____

Discipline your children;
you'll be glad you did—
they'll turn out delightful to live with.
Proverbs 29:17 MSG

January 15

I quickly texted my friend today,
In hopes she'd answer right away,
Instead, I waited, no answer did I see.
I wondered, "Is all okay with her and me?"
Of course, I heard back, all was fine, just a little late.
I am so used to *instant,* it's getting harder to wait.
Yet, it made me stop and think Lord, about me and You.
You listen to all my prayers, and what I'm going through.
Help me not be anxious, when an answer I do not see,
And not wonder if all is okay: You really do care for me.
I need to trust You and wait on Your timing, not mine.
Help me teach my child the same. Let Your light in me shine!

More – See Page

20____ _____ _____
      _____

20____ _____ _____
      _____

20____ _____ _____
      _____

20____ _____ _____
      _____

20____ _____ _____
      _____

20____ _____ _____
      _____

Then he said, "Don't be afraid, Daniel. Since the first day you began to pray
for understanding and to humble yourself before your God,
your request has been heard in heaven.
I have come in answer to your prayer."
Daniel 10:12 NLT

January 16

We like to walk in the cold, crisp air,
Hearing the snow crunch beneath our feet.
We talk, watching white clouds from our mouths.
Then walk again; the silence is so sweet.
A patch of untouched snow beckons us
To stop, and play for a little while.
We plop down, making angels in the snow
Bringing us joy, laughter, and a smile.

More – See Page

20___ _____ _____

_____

20___ _____ _____

_____

20___ _____ _____

_____

20___ _____ _____

_____

20___ _____ _____

_____

20___ _____ _____

_____

"He directs the snow to fall on the earth
and tells the rain to pour down.
Then everyone stops working
so they can watch his power."
Job 37:6,7 NLT

January 17

I say prayers with my sweet children when they go to bed each night.
Then I get busy, check emails, watch TV, then turn off the light.
Lord, help me change my habits. It won't take much for me to do.
Let me end my day with Your Word – praying and focusing on You!

More – See Page

20___ _____ _____
_____

20___ _____ _____
_____

20___ _____ _____
_____

20___ _____ _____
_____

20___ _____ _____
_____

20___ _____ _____
_____

On my bed I remember You;
I think of you through the watches of the night.
Psalm 63:6

January 18

Everyone was created equal,
Yet unique by God.
We need to teach our children
By our loving example
How to see others through His eyes.

More – See Page

20____ _____ _____

20____ _____ _____

20____ _____ _____

20____ _____ _____

20____ _____ _____

20____ _____ _____

So now I am giving you a new commandment:
Love each other.
Just as I have loved you, you should love each other.
Your love for one another will prove to the world
that you are my disciples.
John 13:34,35 NLT

18

January 19

My child did what she was asked to do the very first time.
I gave her a gold star, instead of candy or a dime.
One minute per star is the reward, you see,
For time alone with Dad, or time alone with me.

More – See Page

20____ _____ _____

20____ _____ _____

20____ _____ _____

20____ _____ _____

20____ _____ _____

20____ _____ _____

If you stop listening to instruction, my child,
you will turn your back on knowledge.
Proverbs 19:27

**Download your FREE Parenting Tool for
"First Time Asked" Star Chart at: www.joyinparenting.com

January 20

"Mom likes you best!"
I hear my older child say.
Is there truth in those words?
Do I speak, or act that way?
I can love each child differently,
I can appreciate each unique gift,
Affirming and showing love equally
Giving each one's self-esteem a lift.

More – See Page

20____ _____ _____

20____ _____ _____

20____ _____ _____

20____ _____ _____

20____ _____ _____

20____ _____ _____

My dear brothers and sisters, how can you claim to have faith
in our glorious Lord Jesus Christ if you favor some people over others?
But if you favor some people over others, you are committing a sin.
You are guilty of breaking the law.
James 2:1, 9

January 21

Carpool moms have a captive audience.
Use this unique opportunity to
Listen, laugh, sing, and teach.

More – See Page

20____ _____ _____

20____ _____ _____

20____ _____ _____

20____ _____ _____

20____ _____ _____

20____ _____ _____

Come let us sing for joy to the Lord;
let us shout aloud to the Rock of our salvation.
Let us come before him with thanksgiving
and extol him with music and song.
Psalms 95:1,2

January 22

As I take time to pray with my child as he grows,
I hope he sees prayer modeled and comes to really know
You listen to all his prayers wherever he is, wherever he goes;
Lord, please SHOW yourself to him, he really loves you so!

More – See Page

20___ _____ _____

_____

20___ _____ _____

_____

20___ _____ _____

_____

20___ _____ _____

_____

20___ _____ _____

_____

20___ _____ _____

_____

Whoever has my commands and keeps them
is the one who loves me.
The one who loves me will be loved by my Father,
and I too will love them and SHOW myself to them.
John 14:21

January 23

My daughter wakes a little grouchy today.
No smiles or giggles, she doesn't want to play.
I know what she needs, it just takes a little time
To give hugs and kisses to this child of mine.

More – See Page

20___ _____ _____

_____

20___ _____ _____

_____

20___ _____ _____

_____

20___ _____ _____

_____

20___ _____ _____

_____

20___ _____ _____

_____

I urge you to live a life worthy of the calling you have received.
Be completely humble and gentle, be patient,
bearing with one another in love.
Ephesians 4:1b,2

January 24

When children play together well,
Don't be silent and afraid to break the spell.
Tell them how you like their play,
It brings you joy when they act that way.

More – See Page

20____ _____ _____

20____ _____ _____

20____ _____ _____

20____ _____ _____

20____ _____ _____

20____ _____ _____

Then make me truly happy by agreeing wholeheartedly with each other,
loving one another, and working together with one mind and purpose.
Don't be selfish; don't try to impress others.
Be humble, thinking of others as better than yourselves.
Don't look out for your own interests, but take an interest in others too.
Philippians 2:2,3,4 NLT

January 25

Jesus, you are an example. You showed us how to live,
To love one another and unselfishly how to give.
Please help me be an example to my child every day,
Loving unconditionally in all I do and say.

More – See Page

20____ _____ _____

20____ _____ _____

20____ _____ _____

20____ _____ _____

20____ _____ _____

20____ _____ _____

My command is this:
Love each other as I have loved you.
John 15: 12

January 26

"Please look at me when you talk."
I often say to my children's backs.
"I want to see your eyes, your sweet face,
Whether you're asking a question or telling me facts."
But it made me stop and think.
Lord, do I do the same when I talk to You?
Am I just praying thinking of myself
And not looking at You and all You do?
Help me focus on your faithfulness,
Grace, mercy, wonders, and might;
Your love, character, and forgiveness
Every morning, day, and night.
By gazing at Your glorious face,
During my many ups and downs.
I will find peace, strength, and direction
While training my princesses and clowns.

More – See Page

20___ _____ _____

20___ _____ _____

20___ _____ _____

20___ _____ _____

20___ _____ _____

20___ _____ _____

Look to the Lord and His strength; seek His face always.
Remember the wonders He has done,
His miracles, and judgments He pronounced.
1 Chronicles 16:11,12

January 27

We prayed a long time
Asking God for you.
We shared all our dreams,
And cried to Him, too.
He listened and answered
Our prayerful plea.
That's when He gave you
To your dad and me!

More – See Page

20____ _____ _____

_____

20____ _____ _____

_____

20____ _____ _____

_____

20____ _____ _____

_____

20____ _____ _____

_____

20____ _____ _____

_____

How long Lord? Will you forget me forever?
How long will you hide your face from me?
How long must I wrestle with my thoughts and day after day
have sorrow in my heart? But I trust in your unfailing love;
my heart rejoices in your salvation.
I will sing the Lord's praise, for he has been good to me.
Psalm 13:1,2a,5,6

January 28

"Mom, it's too cold; it's been snowing all day!
Please do not make me go to school today."
But when school is closed, and it's colder still,
Guess who is outside sledding down the hill?

More – See Page

20___ _____ _____

_____

20___ _____ _____

_____

20___ _____ _____

_____

20___ _____ _____

_____

20___ _____ _____

_____

20___ _____ _____

_____

A happy heart makes a face cheerful
Proverbs 15:13

January 29

If there is one thing your child should know,
It's your love is with him wherever he may go.
You may not like what he may say or do,
But let love be constant and forgiving from you.

More – See Page

20____ _____ _____

20____ _____ _____

20____ _____ _____

20____ _____ _____

20____ _____ _____

20____ _____ _____

Above all, love each other deeply,
because love covers over a multitude of sins.
1 Peter 4:8

January 30

God can wash all your cares away,
Just ask Him in. Ask Him to stay.
He'll give you strength, renew your joy,
You'll have more patience for your girl or boy.

More – See Page

20___ _____ _____

20___ _____ _____

20___ _____ _____

20___ _____ _____

20___ _____ _____

20___ _____ _____

Don't be afraid, for I am with you.
Don't be discouraged, for I am your God.
I will strengthen you and help you,
I will hold you up with my victorious right hand.
Isaiah 41:10 NLT

January 31

Shopping in a new grocery store is like
driving in a new town without a GPS.
It's confusing, time-consuming, yet seeing
things you've never seen before.
Take the time: make the effort to show
your child, colors, shapes and sizes;
Open your eyes, have fun, and
make it an adventure to explore!

More – See Page

20___ _____ _____

20___ _____ _____

20___ _____ _____

20___ _____ _____

20___ _____ _____

20___ _____ _____

Open my eyes to see the wonderful truths in your instructions.
Psalm 119:18 NLT

February 1

In our hurry to see the current childhood stage go,
We might miss today's unexpected joys we treasure so.

More – See Page

20____ _____ _____

20____ _____ _____

20____ _____ _____

20____ _____ _____

20____ _____ _____

20____ _____ _____

"If God gives such attention to the appearance of wildflowers—
most of which are never even seen—don't you think he will
attend to you,
take pride in you, do his best or you?
What I'm trying to do here is to get you to relax,
to not be so preoccupied with *getting*, so you can respond to
God's *giving*."
Matthew 6:30 MSG

February 2

Is it almost spring, or some more winter still?
More icicles, or where are the daffodils?
Did the groundhog see his shadow in the snow?
When can I put away the winter clothes? I want to know!
Does it really matter anyway?
Make the most of God's brand new day!

More – See Page

20____ _____ _____

20____ _____ _____

20____ _____ _____

20____ _____ _____

20____ _____ _____

20____ _____ _____

The day is yours, and yours also the night;
You established the sun and the moon.
It was you who set all the boundaries of the earth;
you made both summer and winter.
Psalm 74:16,17

February 3

My everyday dishes do not cost that much.
No special treatment, no place in the hutch.
I have a purpose, I have a good plan,
This way my kids can lend a helping hand.

More – See Page

20___ _____ _____

_____

20___ _____ _____

_____

20___ _____ _____

_____

20___ _____ _____

_____

20___ _____ _____

_____

20___ _____ _____

_____

May the Lord cause you to flourish,
both you and your children.
May you be blessed by the Lord,
the Maker of heaven and earth.
Psalm 115:14,15

February 4

Why do I so worry about all that might be?
I should give it to You, Lord, only You can see.
Please care for him, protect him from the bad out there.
He is Your child before mine, it's Your burden to bear.
I pray daily for Your peace and a settled mind,
Take control of our child, he is one of a kind.

More – See Page

20____ _____ _____

20____ _____ _____

20____ _____ _____

20____ _____ _____

20____ _____ _____

20____ _____ _____

You are my hiding place; you will protect me from trouble
and surround me with songs of deliverance.
I will instruct you and teach you in the way you should go;
I will counsel you with my loving eye on you.
Psalm 32:7,8

February 5

Cage-free, Organic, Non-GMO,
There are so many choices from which to choose.
Cow's milk, Soy milk or Coconut milk,
I am always wondering which is the best to use?
Life seemed to be so much simpler,
When decades ago I was growing up.
I ate what was cooked for the family,
And drank what was poured in my cup.
But with new research, science, and time,
We've discovered new keys to unlock closed doors.
I'll experiment, check for allergies and try them all
To provide the best start for this child of Yours.

More – See Page

20____ _____ _____

20____ _____ _____

20____ _____ _____

20____ _____ _____

20____ _____ _____

20____ _____ _____

She's up before dawn, preparing breakfast
for her family and organizing her day.
She's skilled in the crafts of home
and hearth, diligent in homemaking.
Proverbs 31:15,19 MSG

February 6

Playing tennis off the wall,
Dribbling balls down the hall,
Wrestling with Dad on the floor,
Life with boys sure isn't a bore.

More – See Page

20___ _____ _____

20___ _____ _____

20___ _____ _____

20___ _____ _____

20___ _____ _____

20___ _____ _____

Children are a gift from the Lord;
they are a reward from him.
Psalm 127:3 NLT

February 7

Nurse you,
Rock you,
Hug you,
Hold you.
Teach you,
Train you,
Love you,
Let you. . .
Go!

More – See Page

20____ _____ _____

20____ _____ _____

20____ _____ _____

20____ _____ _____

20____ _____ _____

20____ _____ _____

These commandments that I give you today are to be upon your hearts.
Impress them on your children. Talk about them when you sit at home
and when you walk along the road,
when you lie down and when you get up.
Deuteronomy 6:6,7

February 8

When ice crystals form on a cold window pane
Blocking your view of a snow-covered lane,
Don't scrape them away to see the outside.
Stop and take time to see the beauty inside.
A child's spirit is like a crystal, delicate, and fine,
Growing slowly in all directions, not a straight line.
Anger's heat may melt it, hurtful words can scrape it away.
Appreciate your child's inside, not just his outside today.

More – See Page

20____ _____ _____

20____ _____ _____

20____ _____ _____

20____ _____ _____

20____ _____ _____

20____ _____ _____

And "don't sin by letting anger control you."
Don't let the sun go down while you are still angry,
for anger gives foothold to the devil.
Ephesians 4:26,27

February 9

It's Valentine's week, and if your child asks you:
"What is love? How will I know when it is true?"
I found "love" defined in my favorite Book,
After reading that, there's no place else to look.

. . .continued

More – See Page

20___ _____ _____

20___ _____ _____

20___ _____ _____

20___ _____ _____

20___ _____ _____

20___ _____ _____

If I speak in the tongues of men or of angels, but do not have love,
I am only a resounding gong or a clanging cymbal.
If I have the gift of prophecy and can fathom all the mysteries
and all knowledge, and if I have a faith that can move mountains,
but do not have love, I am nothing.
If I give all I possess to the poor and give over my body to hardship
that I may boast, but do not have love, I gain nothing.
1 Corinthians 13:1-3

February 10

"Love is patient and kind,
No jealousy or envy should I feel.
Never boastful or proud,
Just be unselfish and be 'real'."

. . .continued

More – See Page

20____ _____ _____

20____ _____ _____

20____ _____ _____

20____ _____ _____

20____ _____ _____

20____ _____ _____

Love is patient, love is kind. It does not envy,
it does not boast, it is not proud.
1 Corinthians 13:4

February 11

"Love is not haughty,
Nor demanding of its own way.
It's not irritable or touchy,
To things you may say."

. . .continued

More – See Page

20___ _____ _____

20___ _____ _____

20___ _____ _____

20___ _____ _____

20___ _____ _____

20___ _____ _____

It does not dishonor others, it is not self-seeking,
it is not easily angered. . .
1 Corinthians 13:5a

February 12

"Love does not hold any grudges,
And won't notice when you do wrong.
It's not glad about injustice;
When truth wins, rejoices in song."

. . .continued

More – See Page

20___ _____ _____
       _____

20___ _____ _____
       _____

20___ _____ _____
       _____

20___ _____ _____
       _____

20___ _____ _____
       _____

20___ _____ _____
       _____

It keeps no record of wrongs.
Love does not delight in evil but rejoices with the truth.
1 Corinthians 13:5b,6

February 13

"If you love someone you will be loyal,
And believe in whatever he may do.
Expect the best of him, and defend him;
Then your love will always be ever-new."

More – See Page

20____ _____ _____

20____ _____ _____

20____ _____ _____

20____ _____ _____

20____ _____ _____

20____ _____ _____

It always protects, always trusts,
always hopes, always perseveres.
1 Corinthians 13: 7

February 14

The best Valentine you can give your children
Is to show love, respect, and appreciation for their Dad.

More – See Page

20___ _____ _____

20___ _____ _____

20___ _____ _____

20___ _____ _____

20___ _____ _____

20___ _____ _____

As the scriptures say, "A man leaves his father and mother
and is joined to his wife, and the two are untied into one."
This is a great mystery, but it is an illustration
of the way Christ and the church are one.
So again I say, each man must love his wife as he loves himself,
and wife must respect her husband.
Ephesians 5:31-33 NLT

February 15

Being silent, yet knowing the truth
When you hear a lie that is told,
Is like telling the lie yourself,
Whether you are young or old.

More – See Page

20___ _____ _____

_____

20___ _____ _____

_____

20___ _____ _____

_____

20___ _____ _____

_____

20___ _____ _____

_____

20___ _____ _____

_____

Remember it is a sin to know what you ought to do
and then not do it.
James 4:17 NLT

February 16

A mom's hug and sweet words brings smiles,
Heals hurts, and warms the heart.

More – See Page

20___   _____   _____

20___   _____   _____

20___   _____   _____

20___   _____   _____

20___   _____   _____

20___   _____   _____

Kind words are like honey—
sweet to the soul and healthy for the body.
Proverbs 16:24 NLT

February 17

A child is a gift, a miracle to hold,
God's gift to us, a beautiful gift of gold.
I will learn to protect, to guard, and to defend.
His helpless creation needs more than a friend.
I'll trust and have faith. He will teach me, I know,
How to love and train her in the way she should go.

More – See Page

20___ _____ _____

20___ _____ _____

20___ _____ _____

20___ _____ _____

20___ _____ _____

20___ _____ _____

Train up a child in the way he should go,
and when he is old he will not depart from it.
Proverbs 22:6 NKJV

February 18

I found an old stained recipe card.
It was for my Grandma's special cake.
It's not like today: pour from a box,
Stir in water, then quickly bake.
I'm going to schedule a special afternoon,
With my children 'aproned-up' to measure and mix.
We'll bake Grandma's cake, like I did with my mom.
We'll pass on a family tradition and take some pics!
What else can be passed from generation to generation,
Whether it starts from the past, or maybe it starts with me?
I pray above all else, it will be the influence of my faith.
My love for You and others: please let that be my lasting legacy.

More – See Page

20____ _____ _____

20____ _____ _____

20____ _____ _____

20____ _____ _____

20____ _____ _____

20____ _____ _____

Then we your people, the sheep of your pasture, will praise you forever;
From generation to generation we will proclaim your praise.
Psalm 79:13

February 19

I need to do something just for me:
Take a class, make a craft, something to touch and see.
Diapering, cooking, and working have their place,
But if I don't find something soon. . .I'll be a basket case!

More – See Page

20____   _____   _____

20____   _____   _____

20____   _____   _____

20____   _____   _____

20____   _____   _____

20____   _____   _____

Do not be anxious about anything, but in every situation,
by prayer and petition, with thanksgiving, present your requests to God.
And the peace of God, which transcends all understanding,
will guard your hearts and your minds in Christ Jesus.
Philippians 4:6,7

**To help remember this verse: "When in a Fix, Philippians Four: Six"

February 20

It's snowing hard and my friend calls from the sunny Coast,
Sharing stories of sun and sand, not meaning to boast.
As I wipe up the puddles of snow on my floor,
Grey skies, wet jackets, I could say "Please, NO more!"
But I listen intently, glad for the fun she's found.
For I'll choose to be happy, even with snow all around.

More – See Page

20____ _____ _____
        _____

20____ _____ _____
        _____

20____ _____ _____
        _____

20____ _____ _____
        _____

20____ _____ _____
        _____

20____ _____ _____
        _____

I have learned the secret of being content
in any and every situation, whether well fed or hungry,
whether living in plenty or want.
I can do all this through him who gives me strength.
Philippians 4:12b,13

February 21

Offer your child a few choices today:
What she might do or would like to wear.
Let her see results of her choices,
So later she is not caught unaware.

More – See Page

20____ _____ _____

20____ _____ _____

20____ _____ _____

20____ _____ _____

20____ _____ _____

20____ _____ _____

Do not exasperate your children;
instead bring them up in the training and instruction of the Lord.
Ephesians 6:4

February 22

Just add water and stir.
Tear it open and eat.
Microwave most anything
For a quick and tasty treat.
It's a convenience world,
Everything's instant and fast.
But faith, trust, love take time,
If you want them to last.

More – See Page

20____ _____ _____

20____ _____ _____

20____ _____ _____

20____ _____ _____

20____ _____ _____

20____ _____ _____

Just then a woman who had been subject to bleeding for 12 years
came up behind him and touched the edge of his cloak.
She said to herself, "if I only touch his cloak, I will be healed."
Jesus turned and saw her, "Take heart, daughter," he said,
"your faith has healed you."
And the woman was healed at that moment.
Matthew 9:20-22

February 23

I know a mom who seems to do it all. . .
Work, keep house, she even can play kickball.
To coin a phrase, she's "Supermom" for sure!
Why do I feel so inadequate around her?
Lord, when envy is clouding my vision to see,
Show me the talents and gifts You've given to me.
Then give me the strength, courage, and love I need
To praise and encourage her, then I'll be freed.

More – See Page

20___ _____ _____

20___ _____ _____

20___ _____ _____

20___ _____ _____

20___ _____ _____

20___ _____ _____

Encourage one another daily, as long as it is called "Today"
so that none of you may be hardened by sin's deceitfulness.
Hebrews 3:13

February 24

We're bundled up in the car, the heater slowly warming our feet.
Hats, coats, and gloves on, my children can hardly move in their car seats.
Then we drove by a homeless man, huddled in a corner, lonely and cold.
How can I help him, Lord? Is it safe? How best can I be loving and bold?
We stopped at a fast-food restaurant, for soup, bread, and coffee to go.
Then drove back to Your cold child. I pray he and my children will know. . .
It was You Lord, who made me go and turn my car around,
It was You Lord, who helped me find a blanket for the ground.
We got home and found more coats, hats, and gloves we could share;
Lord, may my children learn by my actions,
not just words, how to love and care.

More – See Page

20____ _____ _____

20____ _____ _____

20____ _____ _____

20____ _____ _____

20____ _____ _____

20____ _____ _____

She opens her arms to the poor and extends her hands to the needy.
Proverbs 31:20

February 25

I'm all dressed up, I have so much to do!
Then the sitter calls, she has a bad flu.
My baby cries, so I pick her right up.
My shirt gets stained from the milk in her cup.
The doorbell rings, and when I open the door,
The dog runs away, can I take any more?
The ads on the Internet say we can do it all,
On days like this one, I would like to give them a call!

More – See Page

20____ _____ _____
_____

20____ _____ _____
_____

20____ _____ _____
_____

20____ _____ _____
_____

20____ _____ _____
_____

20____ _____ _____
_____

I took my troubles to the Lord; I cried out to him,
and he answered my prayer.
Psalm 120:1 NLT

February 26

My toddler is learning from all she touches, tastes, and sees.
But, one day while cleaning the tub and I was on my knees,
I looked up and saw toilet paper like streamers were decorating the hall,
I chuckled, then pulled out my cell, took a photo, and gave my mom a call.

More – See Page

20____ _____ _____
        _____

20____ _____ _____
        _____

20____ _____ _____
        _____

20____ _____ _____
        _____

20____ _____ _____
        _____

20____ _____ _____
        _____

We also pray that you will be strengthened with all his glorious power
so you will have all the endurance and patience you need.
May you be filled with joy, always thanking the Father.
Colossians 1:11 NLT

February 27

At bedtime when the lights are low,
My child shares what bothers him so.
I listen, give a hug, and wipe away a tear,
I tell him how much I love him, and God is near.

More – See Page

20____ _____ _____

20____ _____ _____

20____ _____ _____

20____ _____ _____

20____ _____ _____

20____ _____ _____

I waited patiently for the Lord to help me,
and he turned to me and heard my cry.
He lifted me out of the pit of despair, out of the mud and mire.
He set my feet on solid ground and steadied me as I walked along.
He has given me a new song to sing, a hymn of praise to our God.
Many will see what he has done and be amazed.
They will put their trust in the Lord.
Psalm 40:1,2,3 NLT

February 28

I am feeling overwhelmed with decisions:
Which pre-school and what's the best day care?
Yet, I see moms of teens frazzled with college choices,
Ready to scream and pull out their hair.
Are there scholarships? Will they be accepted?
Then together visit colleges one by one.
Lord, help me focus on today, not worry,
Trust in you and find the daily fun!

More – See Page

20____ _____ _____

20____ _____ _____

20____ _____ _____

20____ _____ _____

20____ _____ _____

20____ _____ _____

Therefore I tell you, do not worry about your life, what you will eat
or drink; or about your body, what you will wear.
Is not life more than food, and the body more than clothes?
Can any one of you by worrying add a single hour to our life?
Matthew 6:25,27

February 29

An extra day. . .Oh Lord, what would You have me do?
How do I make it special, this four-year gift from You?
Do I call a lonely friend, or send her a text or a card?
Do I take time to build a tower or play out in the yard?
Lord, lead me, direct me in Your choice for me today;
I want to make a difference and not throw it away.

More – See Page

20____ _____ _____

20____ _____ _____

20____ _____ _____

20____ _____ _____

20____ _____ _____

20____ _____ _____

Show me Your ways, O Lord; Teach me Your paths.
Lead me in Your truth and teach me,
for You are the God of my salvation;
on You I will wait all the day.
Psalm 25:4,5 NKJV

March 1

The toys clutter the once-clean floor.
Things used to be neat when I walked through the door.
Single days were quiet, predictable but a bore.
I'll choose the mess. . .let's play some more.

More – See Page

20___ _____ _____

_____

20___ _____ _____

_____

20___ _____ _____

_____

20___ _____ _____

_____

20___ _____ _____

_____

20___ _____ _____

_____

A cheerful look brings joy to the heart;
good news makes for good health.
Proverbs 15:30 NLT

March 2

By tickling tiny toes,
Her laughter lightly lifts
The daily dishes drudgery,
She is God's precious gift.

More – See Page

20___ _____ _____

20___ _____ _____

20___ _____ _____

20___ _____ _____

20___ _____ _____

20___ _____ _____

It is good to give thanks to the Lord,
to sing praises to the Most High.
Psalm 92:1 NLT

March 3

Hair combed, shoes tied,
Everyone looks so neat.
Beds made, dishes washed,
I did it! What a feat!
Turn my back, grab my purse,
Crash! Splat! What's that I hear?
Apple juice splattered everywhere,
Lord, give me patience to persevere.

More – See Page

20___ _____ _____

20___ _____ _____

20___ _____ _____

20___ _____ _____

20___ _____ _____

20___ _____ _____

We also glory in our sufferings, because we know that suffering
produces perseverance; perseverance, character; and character, hope.
Romans 5:3,4

March 4

When your child does something that is 'wrong',
Never say, "bad boy," for that's too strong.
Say, "I love you, and what you *did* was bad,
But God made you, and for that I'm glad!"

More – See Page

20____ _____ _____

20____ _____ _____

20____ _____ _____

20____ _____ _____

20____ _____ _____

20____ _____ _____

To learn, you must love discipline;
it is stupid to hate correction.
Proverbs 12:1 NLT

March 5

It's your birthday today! You are growing up so fast!
My baby of yesterday is a big boy at last.
Blow out your candles, may your wish come true.
Mine already has–another year with you.

More – See Page

20____ _____ _____

_____

20____ _____ _____

_____

20____ _____ _____

_____

20____ _____ _____

_____

20____ _____ _____

_____

20____ _____ _____

_____

Praise the Lord. Praise the Lord, my soul.
I will praise the Lord all my life;
I will sing praise to my God as long as I live.
Psalm 146:1,2

March 6

"Not now!" "Don't touch!" "Just go away!"
How often do you say these words each day?
"Okay!" "I'm sorry!" "I love you so!"
Are much better words for your child to know.

More – See Page

20____ _____ _____

20____ _____ _____

20____ _____ _____

20____ _____ _____

20____ _____ _____

20____ _____ _____

I take joy in doing your will, my God,
for your instructions are written on my heart.
Psalm 40:8 NLT

March 7

Breakfast is done! Backpacks are ready!
All are dressed for school from head to toe.
But there's one more thing we regularly do,
We all gather together before we go.
Then I call "Circle Up!"
We all hold hands and pray.
I look forward to these brief minutes
As we start our brand-new day!

More – See Page

20____ _____ _____

20____ _____ _____

20____ _____ _____

20____ _____ _____

20____ _____ _____

20____ _____ _____

Give ear to my words, O Lord, consider my meditation.
Give heed to the voice of my cry, my King and my God,
for to You I will pray.
Psalm 5:1,2 NKJV

March 8

I stumble into the hot shower,
Breathe in the steam and let out a sigh.
The sound and force of the warm water
Sends my little worries good-bye.
I shampoo, singing a praise song,
And soak up the sun's first rays.
I step out refreshed and smiling,
Ready for God's brand-new day.

More – See Page

20____ _____ _____

_____

20____ _____ _____

_____

20____ _____ _____

_____

20____ _____ _____

_____

20____ _____ _____

_____

20____ _____ _____

_____

I will give thanks to you, Lord, with all my heart;
I will tell of your wonderful deeds. I will be glad and rejoice in you;
I will sing the praises of your name, O Most High.
Psalm 9:1,2

March 9

I rock in the stillness just before dawn,
Feeding you, then watching your sweet little yawns.
I'm missing my sleep. I'm tired, that's true.
But this is my favorite time alone with you.

More – See Page

20____ _____ _____

_____

20____ _____ _____

_____

20____ _____ _____

_____

20____ _____ _____

_____

20____ _____ _____

_____

20____ _____ _____

_____

In the morning, Lord, you hear my voice; in the morning
I lay my requests before you and wait expectantly.
Psalm 5:3

March 10

The spilled milk of yesterday is over and done.
Live today with thanks, as if life has just begun.

More – See Page

20____ _____ _____

20____ _____ _____

20____ _____ _____

20____ _____ _____

20____ _____ _____

20____ _____ _____

The Lord is my strength and shield.
I trust him with all my heart.
He helps me and my heart is filled with joy.
I burst out in songs of thanksgiving.
Psalm 28:7 NLT

March 11

When a crocus pops through the last winter snow,
It's God's own way of gently letting us know,
After a winter that's cold, long and dark,
He gives us Spring's hope and earth's new start.
When your world seems so dark, lonely and cold,
Remember the crocus and the Lord's words of old:
"I am with you always!" He has said;
He will give you hope, just ask to be led.

More – See Page

20___ _____ _____

20___ _____ _____

20___ _____ _____

20___ _____ _____

20___ _____ _____

20___ _____ _____

"Teach these new disciples to obey all the commands
I have given you. And be sure of this:
I am with you always, even to the end of the age."
Matthew 28:20 NLT

March 12

When I'm angry, I should take the time
To sit down and count to nine.
Then pray for wisdom, for peace, and grace
When I talk with my child, face to face.

More – See Page

20____ _____ _____
         _____

20____ _____ _____
         _____

20____ _____ _____
         _____

20____ _____ _____
         _____

20____ _____ _____
         _____

20____ _____ _____
         _____

Fools give full vent to their rage,
but the wise bring calm in the end.
Proverbs 29:11

March 13

I was having a tough day today, so decided to give my friend a call.
But it went to *voice message,* so instead, texted her the basics of it all.
Yet, still no answer. Then Lord, you stopped me in my tracks,
Reminding me You're always there, listening. Help me not forget this fact!

More – See Page

20____ _____ _____

20____ _____ _____

20____ _____ _____

20____ _____ _____

20____ _____ _____

20____ _____ _____

Be strong and courageous.
Do not be afraid or terrified because of them,
for the Lord your God goes with you;
he will never leave you or forsake you.
Deuteronomy 31:6

March 14

Lord, help me understand my child today.
Let me hear every word he may say.
Both the words from his lips and also those from his heart,
Being aware of his needs is a good place to start.

More – See Page

20___ _____ _____

20___ _____ _____

20___ _____ _____

20___ _____ _____

20___ _____ _____

20___ _____ _____

Trust in the Lord with all your heart;
do not depend on your own understanding.
Seek his will in all you do,
and he will show you which path to take.
Proverbs 3:5,6 NLT

March 15

As your grandma,
I love showering you with gifts.
I have time to read you a book.
You listen to my long stories.
You don't even care how I look!
I knew that I would love you,
But I didn't have a clue,
Of what joy you'd bring my life,
And how my world now seems so new.

More – See Page

20___ _____ _____
_____

20___ _____ _____
_____

20___ _____ _____
_____

20___ _____ _____
_____

20___ _____ _____
_____

20___ _____ _____
_____

O God, you have taught me from my earliest childhood,
and I constantly tell others about the wonderful things you do.
Now that I am old and gray, do not abandon me, O God.
Let me proclaim your power to this new generation,
and your mighty miracles to all who come after me.
Psalm 71:17,18 NLT

March 16

I buy the food and put it away;
I plan the meals and cook all day!
When the kitchen is clean, and I collapse in a seat,
Then my children ask, "Is there anything to eat?"

More – See Page

20____ _____ _____

20____ _____ _____

20____ _____ _____

20____ _____ _____

20____ _____ _____

20____ _____ _____

Let us not become weary in doing good,
for at the proper time
we will reap a harvest if we do not give up.
Galatians 6:9

March 17

My five-year-old is begging for an iPad© of her own
Rather than her asking for ours as if on loan.
It would be easier I'm sure, to give in to this ongoing request,
But standing firm: creative play and being outside is still the best!

More – See Page

20____ _____ _____

20____ _____ _____

20____ _____ _____

20____ _____ _____

20____ _____ _____

20____ _____ _____

Listen my son, to your father's instructions
and do not forsake your mother's teaching.
Proverbs 1:8

March 18

Sometimes when I get so focused
On my kids, home, and work each day,
I forget to think about my purpose
And following Your plan and Your way.
It is easy to think about my pleasure,
Prosperity and even popularity.
Instead of serving You, praying, listening
To what You want to say to me.
I need to trust you more, to slow down,
And not be constantly on the run.
And then surrender to You saying,
"Not my will Lord, but Yours be done."

More – See Page

20___ _____ _____

20___ _____ _____

20___ _____ _____

20___ _____ _____

20___ _____ _____

20___ _____ _____

He replied to him, "Who is my mother, and who are my brothers?"
Pointing to his disciples, he said, "Here are my mother and my brothers.
For whoever does the will of my Father in heaven
is my brother and sister and mother."
Matthew 12:48,49,50

March 19

"Please use an 'indoor voice,'"
I tend to always say.
But are they copying me
When I yell that way?

More – See Page

20____ _____ _____

_____

20____ _____ _____

_____

20____ _____ _____

_____

20____ _____ _____

_____

20____ _____ _____

_____

20____ _____ _____

_____

Indeed, we all make many mistakes.
For if we could control our tongues,
we would be perfect and
could control ourselves in every other way.
James 3:2 NLT

March 20

Raindrops gently tapping on my window pane,
No loud thunder or lightning, just a light rain.
A day to slow down, yummy soup to cook;
And cuddle with my child reading piles of books.

More – See Page

20____ _____ _____

20____ _____ _____

20____ _____ _____

20____ _____ _____

20____ _____ _____

20____ _____ _____

Be still and know I am God!
Psalm 46:10 NLT

March 21

I put a new T-shirt on my young "three" today,
She asked what the heart in the middle meant to say?
"The heart means "love", so it says "I LOVE You!"
Then I explained, it didn't matter the 'good' or 'bad' she may do.
I told her my love is constant, whether now or when she's a teen.
It's everlasting, like our Heavenly Father's, always kind, never mean.
She smiled with delight, gave me a hug, and ran off to play.
Lord, help me to remember, You love me too in this limitless way.

More – See Page

20___ _____ _____
       _____

20___ _____ _____
       _____

20___ _____ _____
       _____

20___ _____ _____
       _____

20___ _____ _____
       _____

20___ _____ _____
       _____

I have loved you with an everlasting love;
I have drawn you with unfailing kindness.
Jeremiah 31:3

March 22

As I hold you in my arms and watch you sleep,
You're so peaceful, another memory I will keep.
I wish I could capture this feeling, and box it up real tight,
Then store it on the shelf for when my arms are empty at night.
Then some day when I'm alone and feel you don't need me as much,
I'd take down my special box, give thanks, and warm memories I'd touch.

More – See Page

20____ _____ _____

_____

20____ _____ _____

_____

20____ _____ _____

_____

20____ _____ _____

_____

20____ _____ _____

_____

20____ _____ _____

_____

Give thanks to the Lord and proclaim his greatness.
Let the whole world know what he has done.
Sing to him; yes, sing his praises.
Tell everyone about his wonderful deeds.
Psalm 105:1,2 NLT

March 23

I wish I could take this pain from you,
Your fever, cough, and congestion, too.
My heart aches to see you this way.
What else can I do? Sit down and pray.

More – See Page

20____ _____ _____

20____ _____ _____

20____ _____ _____

20____ _____ _____

20____ _____ _____

20____ _____ _____

Devote yourselves to prayer,
being watchful and thankful.
Colossians 4:2

March 24

Keep your cell on the counter
For catching those countless,
Candid, cute keepsakes
Of your cherub, or your clown.

More – See Page

20____ _____ _____

20____ _____ _____

20____ _____ _____

20____ _____ _____

20____ _____ _____

20____ _____ _____

A cheerful heart fills the day with song.
Proverbs 15:15b MSG

March 25

Your child's memory of taking a home-made meal
to a sick friend may last much longer than the
memorized words about love.

More – See Page

20___ _____   _____

20___ _____   _____

20___ _____   _____

20___ _____   _____

20___ _____   _____

20___ _____   _____

Be devoted to one another in love.
Honor one another above yourselves.
Share with the Lord's people who are in need.
Practice hospitality.
Romans 12:10,13

March 26

I am learning that instead of just saying "No"
To a seemingly inappropriate electronic game, or TV show,
I need to sit down, take time, to watch what they see,
Then glance at them as *they* are watching the TV.
How's it impacting them? What scenes, music, words do they hear?
What emotions is it creating? Is it anger, envy, empathy or fear?
Then sitting down together, eating a tasty treat,
I listen, ask questions, as we talk and our eyes meet.
Now, as a parent, a wise decision can be made.
Another building block to better understanding has been laid.
What my children think about and watch, impacts what they will do.
It's my job to keep them focused on serving and honoring YOU!

More – See Page

20___ _____ _____

_____

20___ _____ _____

_____

20___ _____ _____

_____

20___ _____ _____

_____

20___ _____ _____

_____

20___ _____ _____

_____

Finally, brothers and sisters, whatever is true,
whatever is noble, whatever is right, whatever is pure,
whatever is lovely, whatever is admirable—
if anything is excellent or praiseworthy—think about such things.
Philippians 4:8

March 27

You cried tonight.
You said I was unfair,
That I didn't understand,
You thought I didn't care.
But I do understand.
I was young, too.
I care for you so much,
That's why I'm protecting you.
But is protection what you need
At this time in your life?
Or freedom with love,
Discovering life's joys *and* strife?

More – See Page

20___ _____ _____

20___ _____ _____

20___ _____ _____

20___ _____ _____

20___ _____ _____

20___ _____ _____

But the Lord is faithful, and he will strengthen you
and protect you from the evil one.
2 Thessalonians 3:3

March 28

It's okay to give her a hug.
It's okay to miss her, too.
It's okay to say you love her,
For I love my good friend, too.
I know she's like a second mom,
Someone you're glad to see,
Someone you can talk to,
Someone who takes the place of me.
She is a gift to me and you,
A living angel from above.
Our lives are richer knowing her,
Let us thank her for her love.

More – See Page

20___ _____ _____

_____

20___ _____ _____

_____

20___ _____ _____

_____

20___ _____ _____

_____

20___ _____ _____

_____

20___ _____ _____

_____

A sweet friendship refreshes the soul.
Proverbs 27:9b MSG

March 29

I choose to read to my baby today,
She might not understand a thing I say.
But, just in case her young little mind
Is begging to hear words of any kind,
I will read and sing and talk all day,
'Til she talks to me in the very same way.

More – See Page

20____ _____ _____

20____ _____ _____

20____ _____ _____

20____ _____ _____

20____ _____ _____

20____ _____ _____

Sing and make music from your heart to the Lord,
always giving thanks to God the Father for everything,
in the name of our Lord Jesus Christ.
Ephesians 5:19b,20

March 30

Thank you for sitting so quietly today.
Thank you for putting all your clothes away.
Thank you for staying so calm when you wanted to yell.
Thank you for not sharing gossip you wanted to tell.
By taking the time and remembering to thank and praise,
It'll bring you two closer and your child's confidence you'll raise.

More – See Page

20____ _____ _____

_____

20____ _____ _____

_____

20____ _____ _____

_____

20____ _____ _____

_____

20____ _____ _____

_____

20____ _____ _____

_____

Therefore encourage one another and build each other up,
just as in fact you are doing.
1 Thessalonians 5:11

March 31

A glass breaks! And then I hear them cry:
"She did it!" "No, he did it!" is their reply.
I didn't see it. Their word I must take.
My challenge: be fair, loving, no favorites make.

More – See Page

20___ _____ _____
      _____

20___ _____ _____
      _____

20___ _____ _____
      _____

20___ _____ _____
      _____

20___ _____ _____
      _____

20___ _____ _____
      _____

He has shown you, O man, what is good;
and what does the Lord require of you but to do justly,
to love mercy, and to walk humbly with your God?
Micah 6:8 NKJV

April 1

Any time you think you have motherhood mastered,
reality returns!

More – See Page

20___ _____ _____
_____

20___ _____ _____
_____

20___ _____ _____
_____

20___ _____ _____
_____

20___ _____ _____
_____

20___ _____ _____
_____

So, if you think you are standing firm,
be careful that you don't fall!
1 Corinthians 10:12

April 2

Help choose your toddler's tiny friends while you may,
For as a teen, peers help choose what you child might do and say.

More – See Page

20___ _____ _____

_____

20___ _____ _____

_____

20___ _____ _____

_____

20___ _____ _____

_____

20___ _____ _____

_____

20___ _____ _____

_____

Do not be misled:
"Bad company corrupts good character."
1 Corinthians 15:33

April 3

On those days when you do not have an extra ounce to give,
Take a short break and read His Book on how to live.
You will feel renewed, your batteries He'll recharge.
With energy and patience, your problems won't seem as large.

More – See Page

20____ _____ _____

20____ _____ _____

20____ _____ _____

20____ _____ _____

20____ _____ _____

20____ _____ _____

Even youths grow tired and weary, and young men stumble and fall;
but those who hope in the LORD will renew their strength.
They will soar on wings like eagles;
they will run and not grow weary, they will walk and not be faint.
Isaiah 40:30,31

April 4

My baby's ready to start solid foods today.
I've read blogs and books and what they all say.
So many choices in the stores and on the shelf
But I want to find food that she can feed herself.
So, I'll start with God's best that I have found:
Fruit and vegetables, whether on a tree or in the ground.
Avocado, with vitamins and good fats galore,
Then sweet potatoes, no doubt both will end up on the floor.
I know we will have to clean-up. . .face, hands, arms to say the least,
Thank goodness for "Fido," on the floor he will feast.
We will try them all, testing for allergies too, one by one,
It is another new stage, and we will have so much fun!

More – See Page

20___ _____ _____
_____

20___ _____ _____
_____

20___ _____ _____
_____

20___ _____ _____
_____

20___ _____ _____
_____

20___ _____ _____
_____

The land produced vegetation–all sorts of seed-bearing plants,
and trees with seed-bearing fruit. Their seeds produced plants and trees
of the same kind. And God saw it was good.
Genesis 1:12 NLT

April 5

Rocking gently, I sing her a song.
Rocking gently, she'll sleep before long.
This song is the same she hears me sing;
In no time at all, she'll know the same thing.
No matter how tired I am or busy the day,
I repeat this ritual so someday she'll pray,
The Lord's Prayer sung simply from her heart.
What better gift can I give her from the start?

More – See Page

20___ _____ _____

20___ _____ _____

20___ _____ _____

20___ _____ _____

20___ _____ _____

20___ _____ _____

"In this manner therefore pray:
Our Father in heaven, Hallowed be Your name.
Your kingdom come. Your will be done on earth as it is in heaven.
Give us this day our daily bread. And
forgive us our debts as we forgive our debtors.
And do not lead us into temptation, but deliver us from the evil one.
For yours is the kingdom and the power and the glory forever. Amen"
Matthew 6:9-13 NKJV - The Lord's Prayer

April 6

You read to your little sister. You set the table and clean up, too.
You don't even complain too much when you change a diaper or two.
You're sensitive and caring: I can count on you to help me out.
I'm watching my boy become a man; I'm so proud of you I could shout.
You may not appreciate it now, this training I'm putting you through.
But someday, with children of your own,
as a Dad, you'll know what to do.

More – See Page

20___ _____ _____

20___ _____ _____

20___ _____ _____

20___ _____ _____

20___ _____ _____

20___ _____ _____

Start children off on the way they should go,
and even when they are old they will not turn from it.
Proverbs 22:6

April 7

When will there be time just for me?
Time to sit in quiet with a cup of tea?
Yet others say this phase isn't long.
Lord, please help my blues turn to thankful song.

More – See Page

20___ _____ _____

20___ _____ _____

20___ _____ _____

20___ _____ _____

20___ _____ _____

20___ _____ _____

Rejoice always, pray continually, give thanks in all circumstances;
for this is God's will for you in Christ Jesus.
1 Thessalonians 5:16,17,18 NLT

April 8

"I'm here, but tell her I'm not home!"
I instruct my daughter to answer the phone.
But what does my child really hear me say?
Since Mom lies. . .lying must be okay.

More – See Page

20___ _____ _____

20___ _____ _____

20___ _____ _____

20___ _____ _____

20___ _____ _____

20___ _____ _____

The Lord detests lying lips,
but he delights in people who are trustworthy.
Proverbs 12:22

April 9

Sitting together, still and silent,
Listening to the sounds of God's world
May be that special gift you give your child today.

More – See Page

20___ _____ _____
_____

20___ _____ _____
_____

20___ _____ _____
_____

20___ _____ _____
_____

20___ _____ _____
_____

20___ _____ _____
_____

But ask the animals, and they will teach you, or the birds in the sky,
and they will tell you; or speak to the earth, and it will teach you,
or let the fish in the sea inform you. Which of all these does not know
that the hand of the LORD has done this?
In his hand is the life of every creature and the breath of all mankind.
Job 12:7-10

April 10

"Mommy, I need you!" "Mommy, come see!"
Both my children pull at me so anxiously.
Two places at once, how can I be?
Help me be wise, sensitive, and choose carefully.

More – See Page

20___ _____ _____

20___ _____ _____

20___ _____ _____

20___ _____ _____

20___ _____ _____

20___ _____ _____

My brothers and sisters, believers in our glorious
Lord Jesus Christ must not show favoritism.
James 2:1

April 11

Our kids cannot wait to see Grandma and Grandpa today,
Unfortunately, not in person, they live so far away.
Thank goodness for Facetime © that we now use,
Helping us remain close and these relationships not lose.

More – See Page

20____ _____ _____

20____ _____ _____

20____ _____ _____

20____ _____ _____

20____ _____ _____

20____ _____ _____

An elder. . .must have a strong belief in the trustworthy message
he was taught; then he will be able to encourage others
with wholesome teaching
and show those who oppose it where they are wrong.
Titus 1:6a,9 NLT

April 12

One of the biggest challenges of potty training
Is training the mom not to forget!

More – See Page

20____ _____ _____
       _____

20____ _____ _____
       _____

20____ _____ _____
       _____

20____ _____ _____
       _____

20____ _____ _____
       _____

20____ _____ _____
       _____

Carry each other's burdens,
and in this way you will fulfill the law of Christ.
Galatians 6:2

April 13

I gave my child two things of her own,
To unlock the doors of places unknown.
Choosing from things of the world was hard,
But I gave her a Bible and a library card.

More – See Page

20___ _____ _____

20___ _____ _____

20___ _____ _____

20___ _____ _____

20___ _____ _____

20___ _____ _____

Your word is a lamp for my feet, a light on my path.
Psalms 119:105

April 14

I get on my knees to wipe up a spill,
Then on pops my child for a pony-ride thrill.
I am not too happy about the mess today,
But I can change my mood, take a moment to play.

More – See Page

20____ _____ _____

20____ _____ _____

20____ _____ _____

20____ _____ _____

20____ _____ _____

20____ _____ _____

There is a time for everything,
and a season for every activity under the heavens:
a time to weep and a time to laugh,
a time to mourn and a time to dance.
Ecclesiastes 3:1,4

April 15

Six active gifts to give your child:
Time, touching, and talking;
Listening, laughing, and loving.

More – See Page

20___ _____ _____

_____

20___ _____ _____

_____

20___ _____ _____

_____

20___ _____ _____

_____

20___ _____ _____

_____

20___ _____ _____

_____

See what great love the Father has lavished on us,
that we should be called children of God!
And that is what we are! The reason the world does not know us
is that it did not know him.
1 John 3:1

April 16

Sometimes when I'm in the pit of despair,
I wonder if You're listening and really there.
Will You turn my sorrow into something good?
Will I sing your praises where sadness stood?
Then I pray, remembering Your promises to me,
And in time, maybe Your plan for me I will see.

More – See Page

20____ _____ _____

20____ _____ _____

20____ _____ _____

20____ _____ _____

20____ _____ _____

20____ _____ _____

For I know the plans I have for you," declares the LORD,
"plans to prosper you and not to harm you,
plans to give you hope and a future.
Then you will call on me and come and pray to me,
and I will listen to you. You will seek me and find me
when you seek me with all your heart.
Jeremiah 29:11-13

April 17

It's amazing how much grandmothers know
About raising children. . .
Just ask,
And then truly listen.

More – See Page

20____ _____ _____

20____ _____ _____

20____ _____ _____

20____ _____ _____

20____ _____ _____

20____ _____ _____

But correct the wise and they will love you.
Instruct the wise, and they will be even wiser.
Teach the righteous, and they will learn even more.
Proverbs 9:8b,9 NLT

April 18

I want to hug your hurt away.
I want to heal you with my smile.
I want to make you feel better,
Let's just cuddle a little while.

More – See Page

20____ _____ _____

20____ _____ _____

20____ _____ _____

20____ _____ _____

20____ _____ _____

20____ _____ _____

The Lord, Himself, goes before you and will be with you;
He will never leave you nor forsake you.
Do not be afraid; do not be discouraged!
Deuteronomy 31:8

April 19

For a child's trust in you to grow and bloom,
Water it with honesty,
Feed it with consistency,
And shine on it the bright light
Of forgiveness and unconditional love.

More – See Page

20____ _____ _____

20____ _____ _____

20____ _____ _____

20____ _____ _____

20____ _____ _____

20____ _____ _____

Dear children, let us not love with words or speech
but with actions and in truth.
1 John 3:18

April 20

The dishes are piled, the beds aren't made,
But my child really wants me to go out and play.
Lord, remind me gently that dishes and beds can wait,
For in no time at all, my child will be on her way.

More – See Page

20____ _____ _____

20____ _____ _____

20____ _____ _____

20____ _____ _____

20____ _____ _____

20____ _____ _____

Shout joyful praises to God, all the earth!
Sing about the glory of his name!
Tell the world how glorious he is.
Say to God, "How awesome are your deeds."
Psalm 66:1-3a NLT

April 21

I have to capture it all, you are growing up so fast.
I want to remember each moment to make the memories last.
I take photos daily, filling my cell and the iCloud, too.
I need to print them soon, to cherish these cute pictures of you!

More – See Page

20___ _____ _____

_____

20___ _____ _____

_____

20___ _____ _____

_____

20___ _____ _____

_____

20___ _____ _____

_____

20___ _____ _____

_____

Be careful never to forget what you yourself have seen.
Do not let these memories escape from your mind as long as you live!
And be sure to pass them on to your children and grandchildren.
Deuteronomy 4:9 NLT

April 22

"Turn off the lights!" "Don't let the water run."
"Don't throw that away, we'll recycle each one."
"Conserve," "Recycle" are the words we hear today.
But it's Mom who orchestrates these good efforts each day.

More – See Page

20___ _____ _____

20___ _____ _____

20___ _____ _____

20___ _____ _____

20___ _____ _____

20___ _____ _____

So let's not get tired of doing what is good.
At just the right time we will reap a harvest
of blessing if we don't give up.
Galatians 6:9 NLT

April 23

I want to be my child's good friend,
But also a teacher and one to defend.
I want to encourage, love, and praise.
Thank you for this child you've given me to raise.

More – See Page

20____ _____ _____

20____ _____ _____

20____ _____ _____

20____ _____ _____

20____ _____ _____

20____ _____ _____

As a father has compassion on his children,
so the Lord has compassion on those who fear him.
Psalm 103:13

April 24

I've started a new habit that is getting me through my week.
While doing my normal chores I'm praising You, the One I seek.
I praise you Lord, for my children, who get dirty having fun at play.
I focus on their growth and strength, when I'm doing laundry each day.
I praise you Lord, for my children, who are growing tall from food they eat.
I focus on their health, while washing dishes and wiping crumbs off their seat.
I praise you, Lord, for my children, who are finally sleeping thru the night.
I focus on their growing changes, when I'm tucking clean sheets in tight.
By choosing to change my gaze, praising and thanking You in this new way,
I find my load is lighter; I almost look forward to chores each day.

More – See Page

20____ _____ _____

_____

20____ _____ _____

_____

20____ _____ _____

_____

20____ _____ _____

_____

20____ _____ _____

_____

20____ _____ _____

_____

Shout for joy to the Lord, all the earth. Worship the Lord with gladness;
come before Him with joyful songs. Know that the Lord is God.
It is he who made us, and we are his;
we are his people, the sheep of his pasture.
Psalm 100:1,2,3

April 25

Sometimes in my hurry with my long list of things to do,
I forget to stop and listen to these important words from you:
"See my picture!" "Smell my flower." "Please read a book to me."
So, I'll slow down, take the time, because you're my priority.

More – See Page

20____ _____ _____

20____ _____ _____

20____ _____ _____

20____ _____ _____

20____ _____ _____

20____ _____ _____

But Jesus said, "Let the children come to me.
Don't stop them! For the Kingdom of Heaven belongs
to those who are like these children."
Matthew 19:14

April 26

Teachers come in all sizes.
To learn from a child:
Swallow your pride,
Open your ears,
Close your mouth,
And listen from your heart.

More – See Page

20___ _____ _____
        _____

20___ _____ _____
        _____

20___ _____ _____
        _____

20___ _____ _____
        _____

20___ _____ _____
        _____

20___ _____ _____
        _____

Blessed are the meek,
for they will inherit the earth.
Matthew 5:5

April 27

When your child is grown, and gone
And expresses his free will.
Remember you did the best you could,
You loved him and always will.

More – See Page

20___ _____ _____
      _____

20___ _____ _____
      _____

20___ _____ _____
      _____

20___ _____ _____
      _____

20___ _____ _____
      _____

20___ _____ _____
      _____

Love never gives up, never loses faith,
is always hopeful,
and endures through every circumstance.
1 Corinthians 13:7 NLT

April 28

My child:
Notice the beauty of the world out there.
Notice the love and notice those who share.
Notice what you give, and not what you get.
Notice the new student. . .
Maybe a new friend you have not met.

More – See Page

20___ _____ _____

20___ _____ _____

20___ _____ _____

20___ _____ _____

20___ _____ _____

20___ _____ _____

But since you excel in everything—in faith, in speech, in knowledge,
in complete earnestness and in the love we have kindled in you—
see that you also excel in this grace of giving.
2 Corinthians 8:7

April 29

One of the smallest parts of our body
Can cause the most damage
To the spirit of our child. . .
Our tongue!

More – See Page

20____ _____ _____

20____ _____ _____

20____ _____ _____

20____ _____ _____

20____ _____ _____

20____ _____ _____

A bit in the mouth of a horse controls the whole horse.
A small rudder on a huge ship in the hands of a skilled captain
sets a course in the face of the strongest winds.
A word out of your mouth may seem of no account,
but it can accomplish nearly anything—or destroy it!
It only takes a spark, remember, to set off a forest fire.
A careless or wrongly placed word out of your mouth can do that.
James 3:3-5 MSG

April 30

This morning I woke up early, just before dawn.
It was so quiet, poured coffee, to help with the yawns.
Out the window, fog was blanketing all that was there,
Hiding creation's beauty. . .all I could do was stare.
Lord, sometimes my life seems so dark, clouded over with a haze.
It's hard to see You working, when I'm going through this phase.
But the fog disappeared with the rising of the morning sun,
Reminding me. . .
I always see more clearly when putting my faith in Your Son.

More – See Page

20____   _____   _____

20____   _____   _____

20____   _____   _____

20____   _____   _____

20____   _____   _____

20____   _____   _____

Faith is the confidence that what we hope for will actually happen;
it gives us assurance about things we cannot see.
Hebrews 11:1 NLT

May 1

A hand-picked spring flower bouquet
Is a gift of love to brighten your day.

More – See Page

20___ _____ _____

_____

20___ _____ _____

_____

20___ _____ _____

_____

20___ _____ _____

_____

20___ _____ _____

_____

20___ _____ _____

_____

Think how the flowers grow.
They do not work or make cloth.
Yet, I tell you, that King Solomon in all his greatness
was not dressed as well as one of these flowers.
Luke 12:27

May 2

Who has the most influence
On what your child might hear and see?
Is it you, teachers, peers. . .
Or that ever-present TV?

More – See Page

20____ _____ _____
_____

20____ _____ _____
_____

20____ _____ _____
_____

20____ _____ _____
_____

20____ _____ _____
_____

20____ _____ _____
_____

All your children will be taught by the LORD,
and great will be their peace.
Isaiah 54:13

May 3

Today is one of those days I just want to forget!
It was hard to get the kids off to school,
Then driving I got cut off; he was on his cell, I bet!
No cash for lunch,
And wouldn't you know, I left my debit card at home.
I walked by a mirror,
My hair obviously needed a brush or a major comb.
Got a call from school,
One of my children was with the nurse and was very sick. . .
When will this day be over?
While driving to the school I watched the clock slowly tick.
Lord Help!!
I need your guidance from above!
Help me be compassionate,
Slow to anger, abounding in love!

More – See Page

20___ _____ _____

20___ _____ _____

20___ _____ _____

20___ _____ _____

20___ _____ _____

20___ _____ _____

But you, Lord, are a compassionate and gracious God,
slow to anger, abounding in love and faithfulness.
Psalm 86:15

May 4

Sometimes I'm tempted to wish I were someone I'm not.
Sometimes I envy others outwardly or in thought.
Sometimes I do not feel the contentment I should.
Lord, help me to give thanks, for all You make is good.

More – See Page

20____ _____ _____

20____ _____ _____

20____ _____ _____

20____ _____ _____

20____ _____ _____

20____ _____ _____

A heart that has peace is life to the body,
but wrong desires are like the wasting away of the bones.
Proverbs 14:30 NLT

May 5

Wouldn't it be nice
If a mother's kiss
And an Elmo © Band-Aid
Could cure all of our children's hurts?

More – See Page

20___ _____ _____

20___ _____ _____

20___ _____ _____

20___ _____ _____

20___ _____ _____

20___ _____ _____

He heals the brokenhearted and
binds up their wounds.
Psalm 147:3

May 6

A mom is also a child of God.
He will protect, lead, and nurture us, too,
If we just let Him in and ask Him to.

More – See Page

20___ _____ _____

20___ _____ _____

20___ _____ _____

20___ _____ _____

20___ _____ _____

20___ _____ _____

Show me your ways, LORD, teach me your paths.
Guide me in your truth and teach me,
for you are God my Savior,
and my hope is in you all day long.
Psalm 25:4-5

May 7

Praying with your child need not be solemn or hushed.
Praying with your child need not be memorized or rushed.
Pray with your child, from your heart, simple and direct;
Your child will learn from you, and God's love he'll not reject.

More – See Page

20____ _____ _____
_____

20____ _____ _____
_____

20____ _____ _____
_____

20____ _____ _____
_____

20____ _____ _____
_____

20____ _____ _____
_____

Let us go right into the presence of God
with sincere hearts fully trusting him.
Hebrews 10:22a NLT

May 8

Balance every "no" with seven "yeses" and you will find,
A more peaceful home and a child who wants to mind.

More – See Page

20____ _____ _____

_____

20____ _____ _____

_____

20____ _____ _____

_____

20____ _____ _____

_____

20____ _____ _____

_____

20____ _____ _____

_____

A person's wisdom yields patience;
it is to one's glory to overlook an offense.
Proverbs 19:11

May 9

Give yourself a big pat on your back.
Say, "I am doing my best, no matter what I lack."
Just listen to the Lord, do your best to follow through,
For you're raising His precious gifts He has given to you.

More – See Page

20____ _____ _____

20____ _____ _____

20____ _____ _____

20____ _____ _____

20____ _____ _____

20____ _____ _____

I have no greater joy than to hear that my children
are walking in the truth.
3 John 1:4

May 10

I tell my children to patiently wait,
For a treat, their turn, or fun place to go.
They pace and fidget; they whine and plead,
It's not easy to wait, as a mom, I know.
I find I'm often impatient too, Lord,
While I am waiting for my answered prayer.
Sometimes You seem so quiet and silent.
Are You listening? Are You really there?
I am trying to teach my kids patience,
And not give in whenever they cry and plead.
Are You also working on my patience too, Lord?
I'll wait on You! I'll be still and follow Your lead.

More – See Page

20____ _____ _____

_____

20____ _____ _____

_____

20____ _____ _____

_____

20____ _____ _____

_____

20____ _____ _____

_____

20____ _____ _____

_____

Be still before the Lord and wait patiently for him.
Psalm 37:7

May 11

My daughter loves giving me yellow flowers,
Sunflowers, dandelions, anything from the yard.
I treasure each of her gifts. I give them water,
Until they are wilted and time to discard.
Then one time she saved all her quarters and dimes
And went to *The Dollar Store* for something to do.
She bought me a bouquet of yellow silk flowers, saying:
"Mommy, they'll last forever, like how much I love you!"

More – See Page

20____ _____ _____

20____ _____ _____

20____ _____ _____

20____ _____ _____

20____ _____ _____

20____ _____ _____

The grass withers and the flowers fall,
but the Word of our God endures forever.
Isaiah 40:8

May 12

You are special! Find time to discover you.
You are unique! Your gifts are designed for you.
You are a woman, daughter and mother, too.
Find the joy, in whatever you choose to do.

More – See Page

20___ _____ _____

_____

20___ _____ _____

_____

20___ _____ _____

_____

20___ _____ _____

_____

20___ _____ _____

_____

20___ _____ _____

_____

I praise you because I am fearfully and wonderfully made;
your works are wonderful, I know that full well.
Psalm 139:4

May 13

We're teaching our baby sign language,
So she can communicate with ease.
We are learning right along with her,
Hand signs for: "More", "All done" and "Please!"
She is now starting to 'babble."
We research books and our favorite blog.
We're hoping she'll say: "Mama" or "Dada"
But it looks like her first word will be "dog!"

More – See Page

20___ _____ _____

20___ _____ _____

20___ _____ _____

20___ _____ _____

20___ _____ _____

20___ _____ _____

Cultivate these things. Immerse yourself in them.
The people will all see you mature right before their eyes.
1 Timothy 4:15 MSG

May 14

I see other moms teach their children
In ways that are quite different from me.
Lord, help me not judge or be envious.
Help me be the best mom I can be.

More – See Page

20___ _____ _____
       _____

20___ _____ _____
       _____

20___ _____ _____
       _____

20___ _____ _____
       _____

20___ _____ _____
       _____

20___ _____ _____
       _____

Do not judge, or you too will be judged.
For in the same way you judge others, you will be judged,
and with the measure you use, it will be measured to you.
Matthew 7:1,2

May 15

A teenager's bedroom
Is his safety zone,
From the outside world.
The challenge is keeping it
From being a danger zone,
For me to walk through.

More – See Page

20____ _____ _____

20____ _____ _____

20____ _____ _____

20____ _____ _____

20____ _____ _____

20____ _____ _____

Even though I walk through the darkest valley,
I will fear no evil, for you are with me;
your rod and your staff, they comfort me. ☻
Psalm 23:4

May 16

When I am so frazzled and tired, it is so hard to see
Wisdom in handling Your child whom You've entrusted to me.
Help me find rest, and a quiet moment or two;
Please direct my thoughts to focus only on You.

More – See Page

20____ _____ _____

20____ _____ _____

20____ _____ _____

20____ _____ _____

20____ _____ _____

20____ _____ _____

Then Jesus said,
"Come to me, all of you who are weary
and carry heavy burdens, and I will give you rest."
Matthew 11:28 NLT

May 17

Sometimes when I am feeling down,
My kids give my spirits a lift.
Then there are some other times,
I need patience to endure these gifts.

More – See Page

20____ _____ _____
_____

20____ _____ _____
_____

20____ _____ _____
_____

20____ _____ _____
_____

20____ _____ _____
_____

20____ _____ _____
_____

Rejoice in our confident hope.
Be patient in trouble, and keep on praying.
Romans 12:12 NLT

May 18

Love them, pray for them, try your best each day.
Forgive them, play with them, teach them God's Way.
When they get older and ask questions of you,
You can honestly say, "I did the best I could do."

More – See Page

20____ _____ _____

20____ _____ _____

20____ _____ _____

20____ _____ _____

20____ _____ _____

20____ _____ _____

You have been taught the holy Scriptures from childhood,
and they have given you the wisdom to receive the salvation
that comes by trusting in Christ Jesus.
2 Timothy 3:15 NLT

May 19

Start today, please don't wait!
Pray for your child's future mate.

20___ _____ _____

20___ _____ _____

20___ _____ _____

20___ _____ _____

20___ _____ _____

20___ _____ _____

A wife of noble character who can find?
She is worth far more than rubies.
Proverbs 31:10

May 20

Walk in your children's shoes today.
See what they see, feel what they feel.
Then you may come to really know
Their hurts, concerns, and joys are real.

More – See Page

20_____ _____ _____

20_____ _____ _____

20_____ _____ _____

20_____ _____ _____

20_____ _____ _____

20_____ _____ _____

Rejoice with those who rejoice;
mourn with those who mourn.
Romans 12:15

May 21

There's plenty of time to be grown-up.
It's your child's turn to be young.
Take the weight from her tiny shoulders.
Lighten up, Mom, quiet your tongue.

More – See Page

20___ _____ _____

20___ _____ _____

20___ _____ _____

20___ _____ _____

20___ _____ _____

20___ _____ _____

There is a time for everything,
and a season for every activity under the heavens.
A time to tear and a time to mend.
A time to be quiet and a time to speak.
Ecclesiastes 3:1,7

May 22

It's been a long day! All the kids are in bed.
Prayers have been prayed, and books have been read.
I now need a moment, just for me,
To put up my feet, and sip my tea.
The moment will be fleeting, for in no time at all,
I will hear the crumpled clean clothes of the laundry call.

More – See Page

20___ _____ _____

20___ _____ _____

20___ _____ _____

20___ _____ _____

20___ _____ _____

20___ _____ _____

I will refresh the weary and satisfy the faint.
Jeremiah 31:25

May 23

Nursing mothers are an endangered race,
Forgot about often when it's restrooms we face.
We sit on the sink, on the pot if we must. . .
Or on the cold floor with the cobwebs and dust.
All we need is a couch, a chair would do,
To nurse our babies and change them, too.
But my baby doesn't care, so why should I?
Yet, if I can change it, I'm sure going to try.

More – See Page

20____ _____ _____
       _____

20____ _____ _____
       _____

20____ _____ _____
       _____

20____ _____ _____
       _____

20____ _____ _____
       _____

20____ _____ _____
       _____

And this same God who takes care of me
will supply all your needs from his glorious riches,
which have been given to us in Christ Jesus.
Philippians 4:19 NLT

May 24

I'm finally driving alone in the car,
It is quiet and sweet, just God and me!
Suddenly, I felt prompted to turn right at the light.
But now I am NOT going where I'm supposed to be.
I am not sure why He nudged me to make that turn,
But I'm watching and alert with a careful eye,
For even when to me, it does not make any sense,
I've learned to do what He says–His voice not deny.
Then on the sidewalk, a skate-boarder with no helmet
Hits a bump and takes a terrible face-plant fall.
I quickly pull my car over, run to his aid,
Grab my cell and 911 I'm able to call.
I'm so thankful Lord, You interrupted my day,
And I listened to and obeyed Your still, small voice. . .
Thank You, Lord, for letting me be your hands and feet.
At least today, Lord, I believe I made the best choice.

More – See Page

20___ _____ _____

20___ _____ _____

20___ _____ _____

20___ _____ _____

20___ _____ _____

20___ _____ _____

"Master, we've worked hard all night and haven't caught anything.
But because you say so, I will let down the nets." When they had done so,
they caught such a large number of fish that their nets began to break.
Luke 5:5,6

May 25

Unless your teen's outfit is indecent,
Or in extremely poor taste,
Let it be. . .
Or it's precious time you'll waste.

More – See Page

20___ _____ _____
      _____

20___ _____ _____
      _____

20___ _____ _____
      _____

20___ _____ _____
      _____

20___ _____ _____
      _____

20___ _____ _____
      _____

The LORD does not look at the things people look at.
People look at the outward appearance,
but the LORD looks at the heart.
1 Samuel 16:7b

May 26

My child,
I love you no matter what you do,
Where you go,
Or how you feel about me.
I love you no matter what!

More – See Page

20___ _____ _____
_____

20___ _____ _____
_____

20___ _____ _____
_____

20___ _____ _____
_____

20___ _____ _____
_____

20___ _____ _____
_____

But God demonstrates his own love for us in this:
While we were still sinners, Christ died for us.
Romans 5:8

May 27

I love being a mom! It really is a dream come true!
But am I holding back from truly following and obeying only You?
I want to be a living sacrifice offering my whole self to Your call,
But am I afraid You'll send me far away reaching strangers like Apostle Paul?
Do I like being in control and really want *You* to do what *I* say?
Or am I concerned I might look silly? Is it my pride that's in the way?
Lord, please remove any strongholds. Help me trust in you day by day.
You have designed me with a plan and purpose.
Please make it clear, I'll obey.

More – See Page

20___ _____ _____

_____

20___ _____ _____

_____

20___ _____ _____

_____

20___ _____ _____

_____

20___ _____ _____

_____

20___ _____ _____

_____

Therefore, I urge you "sisters" in view of God's mercy,
to offer your bodies as living sacrifices, holy and pleasing to God—
this is your spiritual act of worship.
Romans 12:1

May 28

I don't expect perfection. You don't have to get all A's.
You don't have to win awards, or be a scholar to amaze.
I want you to be just you, and forget about the rest.
Take your time, just give it a try, and do your personal best!

More – See Page

20____ _____ _____

20____ _____ _____

20____ _____ _____

20____ _____ _____

20____ _____ _____

20____ _____ _____

But he said to me, "My grace is sufficient for you,
for my power is made perfect in weakness."
Therefore I will boast all the more gladly about my weaknesses,
so that Christ's power may rest on me.
2 Corinthians 12:9

May 29

My husband and I do not always "parent" the same.
We come from different backgrounds; it's not him I should blame.
God made us unique, with different gifts to use.
I need to value his insight, or his input I will lose.

More – See Page

20___ _____ _____

20___ _____ _____

20___ _____ _____

20___ _____ _____

20___ _____ _____

20___ _____ _____

Two people are better off than one, for they can help each other succeed.
If one person falls, the other can reach out and help.
But someone who falls alone is in real trouble.
A person standing alone can be attacked and defeated,
but two can stand back-to-back and conquer.
Ecclesiastes 4:9,10,12a NLT

May 30

Every soldier who dies for freedom
Is a mother's child.
Let's not take for granted our freedom
For which they died.

More – See Page

20____ _____ _____

20____ _____ _____

20____ _____ _____

20____ _____ _____

20____ _____ _____

20____ _____ _____

There is no greater love than to
lay down one's life for one's friends.
John 15:13 NLT

May 31

Many times I wish I had more hands
To help me through the day.
Evening is the toughest—
Making dinner, helping with homework,
A toddler who only wants to play.
Some call it crazy or "arsenic hour."
I feel it's my own personal test.
I give it to You, Lord–
I am overwhelmed, please hear my prayer,
I need Your guidance to do my best.

More – See Page

20____ _____ _____

20____ _____ _____

20____ _____ _____

20____ _____ _____

20____ _____ _____

20____ _____ _____

O God, listen to my cry! Hear my prayer! From the ends of the Earth,
I cry to you for help when my heart is overwhelmed.
Lead me to the towering rock for safety, you are my safe refuge.
Ps 61:1-3a NLT

June 1

As I tiptoe into your bedroom each night
To pull up the covers and tuck you in tight.
I linger longer just watching you sleep,
And think of our day, and the memories I'll keep.

More – See Page

20___ _____ _____

20___ _____ _____

20___ _____ _____

20___ _____ _____

20___ _____ _____

20___ _____ _____

Give thanks to the Lord and proclaim his greatness.
Let the whole world know what he has done.
Sing to him; yes, sing his praises.
Tell everyone about his wonderful deeds.
1 Chronicles 16:8,9 NLT

June 2

To really love your teenager,
Set her boundaries with love,
Allow her room to grow,
And when it's time,
Let her go.

More – See Page

20___ _____ _____

20___ _____ _____

20___ _____ _____

20___ _____ _____

20___ _____ _____

20___ _____ _____

Lord, you alone are my portion and my cup;
you make my lot secure.
The boundary lines have fallen for me in pleasant places;
surely I have a delightful inheritance.
Psalm 16:5-6

June 3

I tell myself I will find the time
For things that are important to me.
Yet, I feel I am always rushing
And not making the time to see. . .
Little things, like when my child wants me
To just sit and listen to her day,
Or taking a walk, in God's creation,
Sharing with my kids along the way.
Do my kids see me just hurry by,
When I should help someone in need?
Do I ask them to help me cook dinner
For a mom and the child she needs to feed?
Lord, help me make the most of moments
You lay before me every new day.
Help me honor You with my time,
Help me listen, slow down, and obey.

More – See Page

20____ _____ _____

20____ _____ _____

20____ _____ _____

20____ _____ _____

20____ _____ _____

20____ _____ _____

So be careful how you live. Don't live like fools, but like those who are wise.
Make the most of every opportunity in these evil days.
Don't act thoughtlessly, but understand what the Lord wants you to do.
Ephesians 5:15-17 NLT

June 4

When I see my young daughter pretending to be me,
It doesn't seem long ago, I wondered what I would be.
I made many choices, some were good, and others bad.
But You were there for me, and for that I'm so glad.
I need to encourage my child, keep all my motives pure.
Help me be Your example and point out gifts You've given her.

More – See Page

20___ _____ _____

_____

20___ _____ _____

_____

20___ _____ _____

_____

20___ _____ _____

_____

20___ _____ _____

_____

20___ _____ _____

_____

Follow my example, as I follow the example of Christ.
1 Corinthians 11:1

June 5

My little one is weaned: I get my body back!
I gave it my all! Hope there's nothing that she lacks.
Now no more soaked nursing pads, or an unexpected squirt or drip!
No more pumping in the office restroom, before my business trip!
I can eat what I want, like that onion spicy dish,
Or order beer or wine with my favorite meat or fish.
Yet, I still giggle quietly, about that one embarrassing day,
When an officer pulled me over, walking up to my car to say,
"Your right blinker light is out." But by the look on his face, did he see?
I was pumping while driving! Luckily, no ticket this time for me!

More – See Page

20____ _____ _____
        _____

20____ _____ _____
        _____

20____ _____ _____
        _____

20____ _____ _____
        _____

20____ _____ _____
        _____

20____ _____ _____
        _____

She watches over the affairs of her household
and does not eat the bread of idleness.
Her children arise and call her blessed;
her husband also, and he praises her.
Proverbs 31:27,28

June 6

Mom, if you make me feel stupid and small,
I will not have any confidence at all.
Praise and encourage me and see me grow;
My spirit and esteem will then be aglow.

More – See Page

20___ _____ _____

20___ _____ _____

20___ _____ _____

20___ _____ _____

20___ _____ _____

20___ _____ _____

Don't use foul or abusive language.
Let everything you say be good and helpful,
so that your words will be an encouragement
to those who hear them.
Ephesians 4:29 NLT

June 7

As simple as taking the time
To admire a child's catch of the day
Might be today's key for keeping
His ears open to what you say.

More – See Page

20____ _____ _____

20____ _____ _____

20____ _____ _____

20____ _____ _____

20____ _____ _____

20____ _____ _____

Those who are wise will find the time
and way to do what is right.
Ecclesiastes 8:5b NLT

June 8

A child grows best in a climate of love, acceptance, peace, and joy.
Practice this at home. Seek out Godly playmates for your girl or boy.

More – See Page

20___ _____ _____

_____

20___ _____ _____

_____

20___ _____ _____

_____

20___ _____ _____

_____

20___ _____ _____

_____

20___ _____ _____

_____

Pursue righteous living, faithfulness, love and peace.
Enjoy the companionship of those
who call on the Lord with all their hearts.
2 Timothy 2:22 NLT

June 9

There are toys for grownups,
There are toys for a child.
You could spend money daily,
And really go wild.
But inside what do you feel
When the excitement is gone?
Are you sad and depressed,
Or bored and withdrawn?

. . .continued

More – See Page

20____ _____ _____

20____ _____ _____

20____ _____ _____

20____ _____ _____

20____ _____ _____

20____ _____ _____

Still others, like seed sown among thorns, hear the word;
but the worries of this life, the deceitfulness of wealth
and the desires for other things
come in and choke the word, making it unfruitful.
Mark 4: 18,19

June 10

Instead, help those who are lonely,
Care for a child who is sick.
Build a home for the homeless,
Out of love and some bricks.
Share your gifts with others,
Less fortunate than you.
God's the potter, you're the clay,
Let Him mold you in all you do.

More – See Page

20___ _____ _____
_____

20___ _____ _____
_____

20___ _____ _____
_____

20___ _____ _____
_____

20___ _____ _____
_____

20___ _____ _____
_____

Yet you, Lord, are our Father.
We are the clay, you are the potter;
we are all the work of your hand.
Isaiah 64:8

June 11

I am expecting dinner guests within the hour!
There's so much to do, and I still need a shower.
The table is set, oh. . . I need to sweep the floor!
Hope they're not too early knocking on my door.
But in my rush to get everything done,
Tempers flared, and it really wasn't much fun.
But now I remember what I forgot to do,
I first should have spent time alone with You!

More – See Page

20____ _____ _____

_____

20____ _____ _____

_____

20____ _____ _____

_____

20____ _____ _____

_____

20____ _____ _____

_____

20____ _____ _____

_____

As Jesus and the disciples continued on
their way to Jerusalem, they came to
a certain village where a woman
named Martha welcomed him into her home.
Her sister Mary, sat at the Lord's feet, listening to what he taught.
. . .But the Lord said to her, "My dear Martha, you are worried and upset
over all these details! There is only one thing worth being concerned about.
Mary has discovered it, and it will not be taken away from her."
Luke 10:38,39,41,42 NLT

June 12

With tears of gladness, I celebrate this day!
With tears of sadness, he'll soon be on his way.
With tears of pride, I've helped a boy become a man;
With tears of release, Lord, he is now in Your hand.

More – See Page

20____ _____ _____

20____ _____ _____

20____ _____ _____

20____ _____ _____

20____ _____ _____

20____ _____ _____

Acknowledge and take to heart this day
that the Lord is God in heaven above and on the earth below.
There is no other. Keep his decrees and commands,
which I am giving you today, so that it may go well with you
and your children after you and that you may live long
in the land the Lord your God gives you for all time.
Deuteronomy 4:39,40

June 13

Grandparents have a special way
Of taking time from their busy day,
To play a game, or take a walk,
To snuggle quietly, or just talk.
They're not in the hurry I see in myself.
They're not always looking at the clock on the shelf.
Thank You for grandparents, let me learn from them still,
How to slow down, enjoy, and follow Your will.

More – See Page

20___ _____ _____
_____

20___ _____ _____
_____

20___ _____ _____
_____

20___ _____ _____
_____

20___ _____ _____
_____

20___ _____ _____
_____

Wisdom belongs to the aged, and understanding to the old.
But true wisdom and power are found in God;
counsel and understanding are his.
Job 12:12,13 NLT

June 14

Mom, don't tell me what to wear!
Mom, please help me with my hair.
Mom, let me do it and work it through!
Mom, help me. . .please tell me what to do.
Mom, don't touch me, you are in my way.
Mom, I really need your hug today.
One minute it's "Yes!" the next it's "No!"
This, too, will pass: this is how teens grow.

More – See Page

20___ _____ _____

20___ _____ _____

20___ _____ _____

20___ _____ _____

20___ _____ _____

20___ _____ _____

Whoever is patient has great understanding,
but one who is quick-tempered displays folly.
Proverbs 14:29

June 15

It seems like just yesterday
You were my baby, my precious one.
And yet, now you are grown;
Life with your husband has just begun.

. . .continued

More – See Page

20____ _____ _____

20____ _____ _____

20____ _____ _____

20____ _____ _____

20____ _____ _____

20____ _____ _____

Therefore a man shall leave his father and mother
and be joined to his wife, and they shall become one flesh.
Genesis 2:24 NKJV

June 16

I pray for love and laughter,
Ears that listen first, before you speak.
I pray for compromise and compassion,
And that it's Jesus you both shall seek.

. . .continued

More – See Page

20___ _____ _____

_____

20___ _____ _____

_____

20___ _____ _____

_____

20___ _____ _____

_____

20___ _____ _____

_____

20___ _____ _____

_____

But seek first his kingdom and his righteousness,
and all these things will be given to you as well.
Matthew 6:33

June 17

I pray for health and harmony,
That the other's happiness you seek most.
I pray you'll learn to forget and forgive.
Focus on his strengths, for which you can boast.

. . .continued

More – See Page

20____ _____ _____
        _____

20____ _____ _____
        _____

20____ _____ _____
        _____

20____ _____ _____
        _____

20____ _____ _____
        _____

20____ _____ _____
        _____

Bear with each other and forgive one another
if any of you has a grievance against someone.
Forgive as the Lord forgave you.
And over all these virtues put on love,
which binds them all together in perfect unity.
Colossians 3:13-14

June 18

I pray you will always remember
I am your friend, I'll be here for you. . .
To cry to or laugh out loud with
To share all your dreams and doubts, too.

. . .continued

More – See Page

20____   _____   _____

_____

20____   _____   _____

_____

20____   _____   _____

_____

20____   _____   _____

_____

20____   _____   _____

_____

20____   _____   _____

_____

A friend loves at all times.
Proverbs 17:17

June 19

And then, in time, when you're a mom,
With many children of your own,
I pray you will feel as I do. . .
Your children are His gift, on loan.

More – See Page

20___ _____ _____

20___ _____ _____

20___ _____ _____

20___ _____ _____

20___ _____ _____

20___ _____ _____

Children are a heritage from the Lord,
offspring a reward from him.
Psalm 127:3

June 20

It takes effort to be consistent.
It's much easier to just ignore.
But consistency does pays off–-
Reap the benefits when he's four.

More – See Page

20___ _____ _____

_____

20___ _____ _____

_____

20___ _____ _____

_____

20___ _____ _____

_____

20___ _____ _____

_____

20___ _____ _____

_____

Discipline your children,
and they will give you peace;
they will bring you the delights you desire.
Proverbs 29:17

June 21

Your investment of focused,
Unhurried time today
Will yield a return
Beyond your greatest expectations.

More – See Page

20____ _____ _____

_____

20____ _____ _____

_____

20____ _____ _____

_____

20____ _____ _____

_____

20____ _____ _____

_____

20____ _____ _____

_____

Remember this: Whoever sows sparingly
will also reap sparingly,
and whoever sows generously
will also reap generously.
2 Corinthians 9:6

June 22

I can't always stop him when he wants to go.
I can't always stand by him to help him say "no."
I can't always be there in his time of need.
But I can teach him Your Word, and that You'll intercede.

More – See Page

20___ _____ _____

20___ _____ _____

20___ _____ _____

20___ _____ _____

20___ _____ _____

20___ _____ _____

As for God, his way is perfect:
The Lord's word is flawless;
he shields all who take refuge in him.
For who is God besides the Lord?
And who is the Rock except our God?
Psalm 18:30,31

June 23

Did I really hear myself gossiping about a friend today?
Did I share too many details and not in a flattering way?
Lord, please forgive me! Guard my mouth regarding all that I say.
Help me to think before I speak. May my thoughts please You each day.

More – See Page

20___ _____ _____

20___ _____ _____

20___ _____ _____

20___ _____ _____

20___ _____ _____

20___ _____ _____

Set a guard over my mouth, Lord;
keep watch over the door of my lips.
Psalm 141:3

June 24

Before my children go to school or play,
I'd like to get a can of Scotchgard © spray.
Wouldn't it be nice if I could spray them all
To protect them from bullies, bad words, and falls?
Since I cannot, there is only one thing to say,
"Lord, please protect and guard them along their way."

More – See Page

20____ _____ _____

20____ _____ _____

20____ _____ _____

20____ _____ _____

20____ _____ _____

20____ _____ _____

I love you, Lord; you are my strength.
The Lord is my rock, my fortress, and my savior;
my God is my rock, in whom I find protection.
He is my shield, the power that saves me and my place of safety.
I called on the Lord who is worthy of praise,
and he saved me from my enemies.
Psalm 18:1-3 NLT

June 25

I caught myself again talking negatively today,
Not about others, but about ME, what I do and say.
"I'm so stupid!" "I'm a dummy!" "I can't do anything right."
My children and husband hear me. How am I seen in their sight?
Might they start seeing me with those same negative eyes?
Might they start thinking I'm stupid and dumb, instead of wise?

I know You love me, I'm secure, the daughter of the King.
I know You made me smart, caring– I can do most anything!
You didn't make a mistake, when You created who I was to be.
I'm unique, I'm gifted, You gave me all I need to be just me!
Help me take these thoughts captive when they come my way.
Help me remember Your truths and believe in all You say.
I am Your precious child, and my children are Yours, too.
I will rejoice, model what I believe, and fully trust in You!

More – See Page

20___ _____ _____

20___ _____ _____

20___ _____ _____

20___ _____ _____

20___ _____ _____

20___ _____ _____

Take captive every thought to make it obedient to Christ.
2 Corinthians 10:5b

June 26

I can quiet your cries, I can soothe your brow.
By holding and feeding you, as I'm doing now.
We are creating a bond, just you and I,
That God will strengthen as time passes by.

More – See Page

20____ _____ _____

20____ _____ _____

20____ _____ _____

20____ _____ _____

20____ _____ _____

20____ _____ _____

He tends his flock like a shepherd:
He gathers the lambs in his arms
and carries them close to his heart;
he gently leads those that have young.
Isaiah 40:11

June 27

A wise mom knows
When to pull in the reins
And when to let them go.

More – See Page

20___ _____ _____
       _____

20___ _____ _____
       _____

20___ _____ _____
       _____

20___ _____ _____
       _____

20___ _____ _____
       _____

20___ _____ _____
       _____

But the wisdom that is from above is first pure,
then peaceable, gentle, willing to yield,
full of mercy and good fruits,
without partiality and without hypocrisy.
James 3:17 NKJV

June 28

It's summertime–school is out!
The countdown has finally ended,
You can hear all the kids shout!
I am just as excited, too,
But I am much more discreet.
No more carpools and school sports,
I can finally get off the street!

More – See Page

20___ _____ _____

20___ _____ _____

20___ _____ _____

20___ _____ _____

20___ _____ _____

20___ _____ _____

There remains, then, a Sabbath-rest for the people of God;
for anyone who enters God's rest also rests from their works,
just as God did from his.
Hebrews 4:9,10

June 29

An interesting thing happened the other week,
Since raising teens, new teaching tools I always seek.
No matter how often I would repeatedly show them or say:
"When toilet paper is gone, put a new roll on right away.
Be kind to one another, think of them not only you.
This is just a simple, easy task for you to do."
Nothing I would say to them seemed to work,
This kind little chore they all seemed to shirk.

So then one day, a brand-new idea came to my mind.
I would charge each teen a dollar, if an empty roll I'd find.
I would not ask who was the culprit, or who was at fault.
They had to work together for this bad habit to halt.
It only took one time for me to collect a dollar from each one,
Since that day, the problem is solved, a little victory is won!

More – See Page

20___ _____ _____

20___ _____ _____

20___ _____ _____

20___ _____ _____

20___ _____ _____

20___ _____ _____

Love is patient, love is kind.
1 Corinthians 13:4a

June 30

Just because other moms say it's okay,
Doesn't mean it is right, or it is our way.

More – See Page

20____ _____ _____

_____

20____ _____ _____

_____

20____ _____ _____

_____

20____ _____ _____

_____

20____ _____ _____

_____

20____ _____ _____

_____

Enter through the narrow gate.
For wide is the gate and broad is the road
that leads to destruction, and many enter through it.
But small is the gate and narrow the road
that leads to life, and only a few find it.
Matthew 7:13,14

July 1

My child is so busy exploring her world that is so new.
Wanting to touch, taste, see, smell, and climb on a table or two.
I need to be creative when controlling her natural zeal,
And be careful not to crush her desire to learn what is real.
Yet, I will need to set some limits and teach her how to mind.
I'll save the strong NO's for the important and unsafe I find.

More – See Page

20____ _____ _____

20____ _____ _____

20____ _____ _____

20____ _____ _____

20____ _____ _____

20____ _____ _____

Now then, my children, listen to me;
blessed are those who keep my ways.
Listen to my instruction and be wise;
do not disregard it.
Blessed are those who listen to me,
watching daily at my doors, waiting at my doorway.
Proverbs 8:32-34

July 2

What's better than
Frolicking family fun in a
Crisp, clear, country lake
At vacation time?

More – See Page

20____ _____ _____

20____ _____ _____

20____ _____ _____

20____ _____ _____

20____ _____ _____

20____ _____ _____

Then God said, "Let the waters swarm with fish and other life.
Let the skies be filled with birds of every kind."
So God created great sea creatures and every living thing
that scurries and swarms in the water,
and every sort of bird—each producing offspring of the same kind.
And God saw that it was good.
Then God blessed them, saying, "Be fruitful and multiply.
Let the fish fill the seas, and let the birds multiply on the earth."
Genesis 1:20-22 NLT

July 3

We may disagree, but feel free to speak.
Tell me the full story, no matter how bleak.
I'll love you forever, no matter what you do.
There may be consequences, but I'll stand by you.

More – See Page

20____ _____ _____

20____ _____ _____

20____ _____ _____

20____ _____ _____

20____ _____ _____

20____ _____ _____

And I am convinced that nothing
can ever separate us from God's love.
Romans 8:38a NLT

July 4

Let freedom ring from inner cities to mountains high.
Let freedom ring from pastures to towers that touch the sky.
Let freedom ring from the East all the way to the West.
Let freedom ring throughout this land we love the best.
Let freedom ring from my words and actions others see.
Let freedom ring daily, for it's God's desire and decree.

More – See Page

20___ _____ _____

20___ _____ _____

20___ _____ _____

20___ _____ _____

20___ _____ _____

20___ _____ _____

Jesus replied, "Very truly I tell you,
everyone who sins is a slave to sin.
Now a slave has no permanent place in the family,
but a son belongs to it forever.
So if the Son sets you free, you will be free indeed."
John 8:34-36

July 5

I look back to when I said, "I do."
My dreams, my hopes they were all so new.
Candlelight dinners, surprises just for him,
Wearing make-up, and keeping fit at the gym.
But now my children take my energy and time.
Working, dinner, laundry – I'm exhausted at bedtime.
I need to prioritize: I would not want to lose
My husband, our love; Lord, please help me wisely choose

More – See Page

20___ _____ _____

20___ _____ _____

20___ _____ _____

20___ _____ _____

20___ _____ _____

20___ _____ _____

No one has ever seen God;
but if we love one another,
God lives in us and his love is made complete in us.
1 John 4:12

July 6

Sometimes, I look in the mirror and see things
I'd like to change or slightly rearrange.
But then I think of God's handiwork in a snowflake
Or a flower, and babies born each hour.
He has purpose and design with each created babe.
I will stay as I am, for I was custom-made.

More – See Page

20___ _____ _____

20___ _____ _____

20___ _____ _____

20___ _____ _____

20___ _____ _____

20___ _____ _____

For we are God's handiwork,
created in Christ Jesus to do good works,
which God prepared in advance for us to do.
Ephesians 2:10

July 7

My sweet baby and I are scheduled
To take our very first flight alone.
I'm getting nervous, not about my baby,
It's the passengers, their stares, looks, and moans.
I have everything already packed
To feed, diaper, and keep my baby busy.
But thinking of all the, "what ifs,"
Is keeping me awake, making my mind dizzy!
Lord, please help calm my anxious heart.
Show me if there's something more to do.
Wow I have an idea. Thank you, Lord!
This idea came directly from YOU!

More – See Page

20____ _____ _____

20____ _____ _____

20____ _____ _____

20____ _____ _____

20____ _____ _____

20____ _____ _____

Cast all your anxiety on him because He cares for you.
1 Peter 5:7

**Download your FREE Parenting Tool, "Plane Peace"
at: www.joyinparenting.com

189

July 8

Lord, I want my home to be
Peaceful, joyful, a place where we worship You.
I want my home to have
Open doors to my children and their friends, too.
I want my home to remain
A place of love where all children can express
Their worries, hurts, joys, and loves,
A home of acceptance, love and happiness.

More – See Page

20___   _____   _____
      _____

20___   _____   _____
      _____

20___   _____   _____
      _____

20___   _____   _____
      _____

20___   _____   _____
      _____

20___   _____   _____
      _____

Most important of all,
continue to show deep love for each other,
for love covers a multitude of sins.
Cheerfully share your home with those who need
a meal or a place to stay.
1 Peter 4:8,9 NLT

July 9

They say I radiate, and I guess I do.
I feel good: I'm excited just waiting for you.
A feeling of expectancy, never knew what that meant. . .
Like, "waiting impatiently" for the miracle God has sent.
I feel like I am special, and God has chosen me
To nurture His creation before all get to see. . .
His work of art that's taking only nine months to create;
He's using me daily, I guess that's why I radiate.

More – See Page

20____ _____ _____

20____ _____ _____

20____ _____ _____

20____ _____ _____

20____ _____ _____

20____ _____ _____

A few days later Mary hurried to the hill country of Judea, to the town
where Zechariah lived. She entered the house and greeted Elizabeth.
At the sound of Mary's greeting, Elizabeth's child leaped within her,
and Elizabeth was filled with the Holy Spirit.
"When I heard your greeting, the baby in my womb jumped for joy.
You are blessed because you believed that the Lord would do
what he said."
Luke 1:39-41,44,45 NLT

July 10

My child fell today, but hardly a scratch I see.
Yet, by her tears you would think she'd broken her knee.
I want to say, "Stop crying, it is really not that bad!"
But compassion wins, "I bet it hurts, no wonder you're sad."
I change the subject and show her something else to play,
And in no time at all, the hurt has gone away.

More – See Page

20____ _____ _____

20____ _____ _____

20____ _____ _____

20____ _____ _____

20____ _____ _____

20____ _____ _____

My brother and sisters, take note of this:
Everyone should be quick to listen,
slow to speak and slow to become angry.
James 1:19

July 11

As the waves wash away
My child's castle of sand,
It reminds me our foundation
Should be laid by God's Word and hand.

More – See Page

20___ _____ _____
_____

20___ _____ _____
_____

20___ _____ _____
_____

20___ _____ _____
_____

20___ _____ _____
_____

20___ _____ _____
_____

"Therefore everyone who hears these words of mine and
puts them into practice is like a wise man who built his house on the rock.
But everyone who hears these words of mine and does not
put them into practice is like a foolish man who built his house on sand.
The rain came down, the streams rose, and the winds blew
and beat against that house, and it fell with a great crash."
Matthew 7:24,26,27

July 12

I try to follow the Golden Rule.
I teach my children to do the same.
I know how I want to be treated,
Yet, when I treat others poorly, I'm to blame.
It's easy to treat others nicely,
When they are nice and look like me.
But when others are mean-spirited and hateful,
Jesus still calls me to love, even my enemy.
This kind of love isn't natural or easy,
Especially when people are so unkind.
In fact, it is nearly impossible; however,
The Holy Spirit is the power source I can find.

More – See Page

20____ _____ _____

20____ _____ _____

20____ _____ _____

20____ _____ _____

20____ _____ _____

20____ _____ _____

You have heard the law that says,
'Love your neighbor and hate your enemy.'
But I say, love your enemies! Pray for those who persecute you!
In that way, you will be acting as true children of your Father in heaven.
Matthew 5:43,44 45a NLT

July 13

No matter how frustrated and angry you may be,
Do not say "I'll leave you if you don't come now with me!"
You know you wouldn't do it. You know it is not true.
Think of a better solution that works for both of you.

More – See Page

20___ _____ _____

20___ _____ _____

20___ _____ _____

20___ _____ _____

20___ _____ _____

20___ _____ _____

Therefore, each of you must put off falsehood
and speak truthfully to your neighbor,
for we are all members of one body.
"In your anger do not sin."
Ephesians 4:25,26a

July 14

Sometimes their music may be too loud in your ears.
Sometimes their clothes may make you want to laugh to tears.
Sometimes their slang words may seem a little bit strange.
Think back when you were a teen, your outlook may change.

More – See Page

20____ _____ _____

_____

20____ _____ _____

_____

20____ _____ _____

_____

20____ _____ _____

_____

20____ _____ _____

_____

20____ _____ _____

_____

"Why do you look at the speck of sawdust in your brother's eye
and pay no attention to the plank in your own eye?
How can you say to your brother,
'Brother, let me take the speck out of your eye,'
when you yourself fail to see the plank in your own eye?
You hypocrite, first take the plank out of your eye,
and then you will see clearly to remove the speck from your
brother's eye."
Luke 6:41,42

July 15

Vacations can be fun,
But it's tiring, just preparing for one. . ..
What to bring? What still to do?
What to wash? What to buy new?
What to pack? What to save for the road?
I need a vacation from planning this vacation
Or, I might just act like a little kid and explode!

More – See Page

20____ _____ _____

20____ _____ _____

20____ _____ _____

20____ _____ _____

20____ _____ _____

20____ _____ _____

The end of a matter is better than its beginning,
and patience is better than pride.
Ecclesiastes 7:8

July 16

Each day is a series of special moments,
Some hidden, others so clear.
Discover and treasure these moments
And hold those you love so near.

More – See Page

20___ _____ _____

_____

20___ _____ _____

_____

20___ _____ _____

_____

20___ _____ _____

_____

20___ _____ _____

_____

20___ _____ _____

_____

Praise the Lord, my soul;
all my inmost being, praise his holy name.
Praise the Lord, my soul,
and forget not all his benefits—
Psalm 103:1,2

July 17

Do you want the blue or green one?
Do you want to go outside and play?
Asking your child's opinion
Has its proper place each day.
But when it gets out of balance
And your *child* is in control,
It's time to teach and tell with love
To re-gain your parental role.

More – See Page

20___ _____ _____

20___ _____ _____

20___ _____ _____

20___ _____ _____

20___ _____ _____

20___ _____ _____

If you reject discipline, you only harm yourself;
but if you listen to correction,
you grow in understanding.
Proverbs 15:32 NLT

July 18

I was feeding my newborn in the middle of the night
Sleep deprived, but happy, I love just holding her so tight.
I was staring at this miracle so perfect in every way,
A masterpiece the Lord created, as if He wanted to say:
"I have designed her with a plan and purpose, as you are too!
I already know in advance all the good works she will do."
I look forward to teaching her all the many truths about You.
Your love, wisdom, forgiveness, and many, mighty miracles too.
So someday when she's older, she'll ask You to come in and rule her life,
Receiving this gift of love from You to guide her days of joy and strife.
I want to make sure that she knows, she is not saved BY the works she will do,
But because she is saved, she will WANT to do good works in love to honor You.

More – See Page

20____ _____ _____

_____

20____ _____ _____

_____

20____ _____ _____

_____

20____ _____ _____

_____

20____ _____ _____

_____

20____ _____ _____

_____

God saved you by his grace when you believed.
And you can't take credit for this; it is a gift from God.
Salvation is not a reward for the good things we have done,
so none of us can boast about it. For we are God's masterpiece.
He has created us anew in Christ Jesus,
so we can do the good things he planned for us long ago.
Ephesians 2:8,9,10 NLT

July 19

Now that my children are all teens,
There is one privilege I love to do.
It's serving as the mom on mission trips.
I learn, and I am challenged, too!
It is a joy to watch all the teens change
When serving others for a week.
Right before my eyes their hearts grow,
Focused on Jesus, His will they now seek.

More – See Page

20___ _____ _____

20___ _____ _____

20___ _____ _____

20___ _____ _____

20___ _____ _____

20___ _____ _____

When you help someone out,
don't think about how it looks.
Just do it—quietly and unobtrusively.
That is the way your God, who conceived you in love,
working behind the scenes, helps you out.
Matthew 6:3,4 MSG

July 20

Peanut butter on the countertop,
Strawberry jam dripping to the floor.
I teach my teen to take care of himself,
But at clean-up time, he is out the door!

More – See Page

20___ _____ _____

20___ _____ _____

20___ _____ _____

20___ _____ _____

20___ _____ _____

20___ _____ _____

Whatever you do,
work at it with all your heart,
as working for the Lord,
not for human masters.
Colossians 3:23

July 21

Isn't it funny how as a little girl
I couldn't wait
To put on my mom's high heels,
But as a grownup
I can't wait to take them off?

More – See Page

20___ _____ _____

20___ _____ _____

20___ _____ _____

20___ _____ _____

20___ _____ _____

20___ _____ _____

Charm is deceptive,
and beauty does not last;
but a woman who fears the Lord
will be greatly praised.
Proverbs 31:30

July 22

Selling lemonade in the hot summer sun
To friends passing by, can be so much fun.
I remember doing this same summer thing,
I'd sit for hours, in the quiet, I'd sing.
Some childhood memories are re-lived for me,
While watching my child enjoy life, so carefree.

More – See Page

20___ _____ _____

_____

20___ _____ _____

_____

20___ _____ _____

_____

20___ _____ _____

_____

20___ _____ _____

_____

20___ _____ _____

_____

Sing praises over everything,
any excuse for a song to God the Father
in the name of our Master, Jesus Christ.
Ephesians 5:19,20 MSG

July 23

If a child seems deaf to what you may say,
Look at the message in your words today.
Do you correct and order him about?
Do you talk above, beneath: do you shout?
Sit down together face-to-face,
Ask forgiveness for being "on his case."
Listen, ask questions, show him gentle care.
His ears will open, ask Jesus in prayer.

More – See Page

20____ _____ _____

20____ _____ _____

20____ _____ _____

20____ _____ _____

20____ _____ _____

20____ _____ _____

Fools think their own way is right,
but the wise listen to others.
Proverbs 12:15 NLT

July 24

No matter how much you think you will remember
How a newborn will alter your life,
When it happens,
It's obvious you've forgotten.

More – See Page

20____ _____ _____

_____

20____ _____ _____

_____

20____ _____ _____

_____

20____ _____ _____

_____

20____ _____ _____

_____

20____ _____ _____

_____

Give your entire attention to what God is doing right now,
and don't get worked up about
what may or may not happen tomorrow.
God will help you deal with whatever hard things
come up when the time comes.
Matthew 6:34 MSG

July 25

As our children grow before our eyes,
We need to loosen our love ties.

More – See Page

20___ _____ _____

20___ _____ _____

20___ _____ _____

20___ _____ _____

20___ _____ _____

20___ _____ _____

The wise are known for their understanding,
and pleasant words are persuasive.
Proverbs 16:21 NLT

July 26

Two's and teens are similar. . .
I find they both need:
Boundaries with flexible fences,
My time and my tender love,
Persistency and consistency,
And all His help from above.

More – See Page

20____ _____ _____

20____ _____ _____

20____ _____ _____

20____ _____ _____

20____ _____ _____

20____ _____ _____

Summing up:
Be agreeable, be sympathetic, be loving,
be compassionate, be humble.
That goes for all of you, no exceptions.
No retaliation. No sharp-tongued sarcasm.
Instead, bless—that's your job, to bless.
You'll be a blessing and also get a blessing.
1 Peter 3:8-12 MSG

July 27

Use me, show me the way,
To be the best mom I can be today.
I am Yours! You made me!
Lord, please use me today!

You are my Savior, my Lord, and the Way,
You died for my sins, I'm free today!
I am yours, You made me,
Lord, please use me today!

More – See Page

20___ _____ _____

20___ _____ _____

20___ _____ _____

20___ _____ _____

20___ _____ _____

20___ _____ _____

Jesus told him, "I am the way, the truth and the life.
No one can come to the Father except through me.
I tell you the truth, anyone who believes in me
will do the same works I have done, and even greater works,
because I am going to be with the Father.
You can ask for anything in my name, and I will do it,
so that the Son can bring glory to the Father."
John 14: 6,2,13 NLT

July 28

Often a child's creativity appears
When the TV, laptop, cell
And scheduled activities disappear.

More – See Page

20___ _____ _____

20___ _____ _____

20___ _____ _____

20___ _____ _____

20___ _____ _____

20___ _____ _____

He has filled him with the Spirit of God,
with wisdom, with understanding, with knowledge
and with all kinds of skills—to make artistic designs,
for work in gold, silver and bronze, to cut and set stones,
to work in wood and to engage in all kinds of artistic crafts.
Exodus 35:31-33

July 29

When God made the motor for toddlers,
There is one thing He forgot, I fear.
Often, the throttle gets stuck on high,
For he forgot to include low gear!
Yet, isn't that what I love the most
Watching my little one laugh and play?
Surely it keeps me in better shape,
Lord, thank you for this blessing today!

More – See Page

20___ _____ _____

20___ _____ _____

20___ _____ _____

20___ _____ _____

20___ _____ _____

20___ _____ _____

O Lord my God,
you have performed many wonders for us.
Your plans for us are too numerous to list.
You have no equal.
If a tried to recite all your wonderful deeds,
I would never come to the end of them.
Psalm 40:5 NLT

July 30

When we take them only to the extraordinary,
The spectacular, and the amazing too,
Our children can lose the awe
Of simple creations designed by You.

More – See Page

20___ _____ _____
_____

20___ _____ _____
_____

20___ _____ _____
_____

20___ _____ _____
_____

20___ _____ _____
_____

20___ _____ _____
_____

Stop and consider the wonderful miracles of God!
Do you know how God controls the storm
and causes the lightning to flash from the clouds?
Do you understand how he moves the clouds
with wonderful perfection and skill?
No wonder people everywhere fear him.
All who are wise show him reverence.
Job 37:14,15,16,24 NLT

July 31

When you are tired, exhausted,
Feeling no one seems to care!
Get on your knees and cry out to Him.
He's always listening, always there.

More – See Page

20___ _____   _____

20___ _____   _____

20___ _____   _____

20___ _____   _____

20___ _____   _____

20___ _____   _____

Rise during the night and cry out.
Pour out your hearts like water to the Lord.
Lift up your hands to him in prayer,
pleading for your children.
Lamentations 2:19 NLT

August 1

I'm standing in line at the grocery store
With no children in my arms or cart.
Yet, I still find myself so gently swaying.
Smiling, I still rock them in my heart.

More – See Page

20____ _____ _____

20____ _____ _____

20____ _____ _____

20____ _____ _____

20____ _____ _____

20____ _____ _____

A longing fulfilled is sweet to the soul.
Proverbs 13:19a

August 2

Sometimes we might think we know
what our child might do or say.
But listen to what your child says. . .
not to what you think he may say.

More – See Page

20___ _____ _____

_____

20___ _____ _____

_____

20___ _____ _____

_____

20___ _____ _____

_____

20___ _____ _____

_____

20___ _____ _____

_____

Commit yourself to instruction;
listen carefully to words of knowledge.
Proverbs 23:12 NLT

August 3

You two can disagree
And respectfully express what you think.
But remember your brother is your friend,
You'll always have that forever love link.

More – See Page

20___ _____ _____

20___ _____ _____

20___ _____ _____

20___ _____ _____

20___ _____ _____

20___ _____ _____

Love each other with genuine affection,
and take delight in honoring each other.
Romans 12:10

August 4

Thank you for my children!
They are such gifts to me.
Thank you for their laughs and giggles,
Through their eyes I more clearly see.
Thank you for their little fights,
They give me a chance to teach.
Thank you for unexpected fears and hurts,
Then together it's You we both will reach.

More – See Page

20____ _____ _____

20____ _____ _____

20____ _____ _____

20____ _____ _____

20____ _____ _____

20____ _____ _____

Give thanks in all circumstances;
for this is God's will for you
in Christ Jesus.
1 Thessalonians 5:18

August 5

My friend and her family are moving,
Not nearby, but out of the state.
I have treasured all our walks and lunches,
And our numerous coffee dates.
I'll miss our sweet conversations,
And praying with her so often, too.
She understands who I really am,
And listens to all I'm going through.
I know we'll text, send emails,
And have many talks on the phone.
But there is nothing like a good friend -
Who loves you, so you don't feel all alone.
But daily You remind me, I'm not alone.
You're not only my Savior, but my friend too.
I don't need my cell or other electronics,
I can talk any time, any day, with You.

More – See Page

20___ _____ _____

_____

20___ _____ _____

_____

20___ _____ _____

_____

20___ _____ _____

_____

20___ _____ _____

_____

20___ _____ _____

_____

You are my friends if you do what I command.
I no longer call you servants, because a servant
does not know his master's business.
Instead I have called you friends, for everything that I learned
from my Father I have made known to you.
John 15:14,15

August 6

"Are we there yet?" is the traveling cry.
"Are we there yet?" I take a deep sigh.
"Are we there yet?" The time passes so slow.
Are vacations worth the effort? . . .
When we get there, I'll let you know.

More – See Page

20___ _____ _____

20___ _____ _____

20___ _____ _____

20___ _____ _____

20___ _____ _____

20___ _____ _____

We also pray that you will be strengthened
with all His glorious power
so you will have all the endurance
and patience you need. May you be filled with joy.
Colossians 1:11

August 7

I'm feeling so tired, no energy, no pep.
I do not want to get up or take one more step.
I have my crackers on the table by my bed,
Yet the thought of any food is something I dread.
But I need to eat, to help my baby grow.
I need strength for my others; they need me, I know.
The thought of my sweethearts makes me sit up tall,
Then slowly take slippered steps down the hall.
To the kitchen I will go, which is not my favorite sight.
I've got to think more positive and set my attitude right.
I will eat good food, and I will try to keep it down.
This trimester's soon over; come on smiles, goodbye frowns.

More – See Page

20___ _____ _____

20___ _____ _____

20___ _____ _____

20___ _____ _____

20___ _____ _____

20___ _____ _____

Then Jesus said, "Come to me,
all of you who are weary
and carry heavy burdens,
and I will give you rest."
Matthew 11:28

August 8

Often I look for shortcuts,
In the things I choose to do.
But there is no shortcut to be found,
When I'm quietly listening to You.

More – See Page

20____ _____ _____
       _____

20____ _____ _____
       _____

20____ _____ _____
       _____

20____ _____ _____
       _____

20____ _____ _____
       _____

20____ _____ _____
       _____

Be still and know that I am God!
Psalm 46:10a

August 9

You got your first goal today!
We all let out screams and shouts!
You practiced and worked hard,
To that there is no doubt.
Enjoy the praise and accolades,
YOU did it. . .or so it may seem.
But remember, give thanks, praise others,
For you are only ONE part of the whole team!

More – See Page

20___ _____ _____

20___ _____ _____

20___ _____ _____

20___ _____ _____

20___ _____ _____

20___ _____ _____

Don't be selfish; don't try to impress others.
Be humble, thinking of others as better than yourselves.
Don't look out only for your own interests,
but take an interest in others, too.
Philippians 2:3,4 NLT

August 10

"Mommy!!"
My child cries from a bad dream in her sleep.
I hurry to her bed, hugging and holding her.
She is now breathing calmly and not a peep.
I'm so glad she now feels so safe
When she's cuddled in my warm arms.
In no time at all, she'll fall asleep
'Till sunrise or morning alarms.
But as I hold my sleeping child,
My thoughts turn to think about You.
When I'm worried, stressed, or scared,
It's Your arms I need to run to.

More – See Page

20___ _____ _____

_____

20___ _____ _____

_____

20___ _____ _____

_____

20___ _____ _____

_____

20___ _____ _____

_____

20___ _____ _____

_____

The name of the Lord is a strong tower;
The righteous run to it and are safe.
Proverbs 18:10 NKJV

August 11

Sometimes a child doesn't need a nap
As much as a mother needs a break.

More – See Page

20___ _____ _____

_____

20___ _____ _____

_____

20___ _____ _____

_____

20___ _____ _____

_____

20___ _____ _____

_____

20___ _____ _____

_____

The Lord replied,
"My Presence will go with you,
and I will give you rest."
Exodus 33:14

August 12

Turn off the TV.
Pull out the lawn chair.
Sit under the stars.
Breathe in the night air.
Listen to the night sounds,
See a falling star or two.
God doesn't make reruns.
Every night is brand new.

More – See Page

20___ _____ _____

20___ _____ _____

20___ _____ _____

20___ _____ _____

20___ _____ _____

20___ _____ _____

The Heavens declare the glory of God;
the skies proclaim the work of His hands.
Day after day they pour forth speech;
night after night they reveal knowledge.
They have no speech, they use no words;
no sound is heard from them.
Yet their voice goes out into all the earth,
their words to the ends of the world.
Psalm 19:1-4

August 13

I try to teach my child what's right and wrong
In my deeds, my words, and even in song.
But the Web, in music, TV and the rest,
They say, "It might seem wrong, but it is the best."
Please give my child strength to do what is right in Your eyes,
Help him say "no" to wrong, and let him be godly wise.

More – See Page

20____ _____ _____

20____ _____ _____

20____ _____ _____

20____ _____ _____

20____ _____ _____

20____ _____ _____

Truthful words stand the test of time,
but lies are soon exposed.
Proverbs 12:19 NLT

August 14

Why is it over summer vacation
My child's reasoning skills
Also take a break?

More – See Page

20___ _____   _____
      _____

20___ _____   _____
      _____

20___ _____   _____
      _____

20___ _____   _____
      _____

20___ _____   _____
      _____

20___ _____   _____
      _____

My child, if your heart is wise,
my own heart will rejoice!
Everything in me will celebrate
when you speak what is right.
Proverbs 23:15,16 NLT

August 15

I have been wronged
By someone I call my friend.
Lord, help me forgive, show love,
And my friendship still extend.

More – See Page

20___ _____ _____

20___ _____ _____

20___ _____ _____

20___ _____ _____

20___ _____ _____

20___ _____ _____

Do not judge,
and you will not be judged.
Do not condemn,
and you will not be condemned.
Forgive,
and you will be forgiven.
Luke 6:37

August 16

One of your children may be just like you,
Thinking, acting, feeling as you do.
Another may be your opposite in many ways,
Causing numerous, challenging, frustrating days!
Yet, we are asked to give love, and be fair,
To love each equally and show we care.
We cannot take sides or a favorite choose,
For in the process, a child's spirit we'll lose.

More – See Page

20____ _____ _____

20____ _____ _____

20____ _____ _____

20____ _____ _____

20____ _____ _____

20____ _____ _____

Love makes up for all offenses.
Proverbs 10:12b NLT

August 17

Lord, help me keep my priorities straight,
First comes You, all else can wait.

More – See Page

20____ _____ _____

_____

20____ _____ _____

_____

20____ _____ _____

_____

20____ _____ _____

_____

20____ _____ _____

_____

20____ _____ _____

_____

You are my witnesses.
Is there any God besides me?
No, there is no other Rock;
I know not one.
Isaiah 44:8b

August 18

Wouldn't you know it, we're in a big store,
My "two" throws a tantrum. "Yikes! Where's the door?"
A voice inside me says: "Be calm and pray.
Stop what you are doing, lead her away."
We walk to a corner. I hug her tight.
I review the rules: we'll not yell or fight.
Is she tired? Hungry? Wrong time of the day?
Please give me wisdom for our next getaway.

More – See Page

20___ _____ _____
       _____

20___ _____ _____
       _____

20___ _____ _____
       _____

20___ _____ _____
       _____

20___ _____ _____
       _____

20___ _____ _____
       _____

Devote yourselves to prayer
with an alert mind and a thankful heart.
Let your conversation be gracious and attractive
so that you will have the right response for everyone.
Colossians 4:2,6 NLT

August 19

It's surprising how a teenage girl will share it all,
During a quiet lunch and a walk through a mall.

More – See Page

20___ _____ _____

20___ _____ _____

20___ _____ _____

20___ _____ _____

20___ _____ _____

20___ _____ _____

For whatever is in your heart
determines what you say.
A good person produces good things
from the treasury of a good heart.
Matthew 12:34b,35a NLT

August 20

When you feel alone and down,
You deserve a lift, that's true.
Take time to pray, then call another mom
Who understands what you're going through.

More – See Page

20____ _____ _____
         _____

20____ _____ _____
         _____

20____ _____ _____
         _____

20____ _____ _____
         _____

20____ _____ _____
         _____.

20____ _____ _____
         _____

Each one of us needs to look after the good
of the people around us, asking ourselves,
"How can I help?" That's exactly what Jesus did.
He didn't make it easy for himself by avoiding people's troubles,
but waded right in and helped out.
Romans 15:2,3 MSG

August 21

Let your child grow and let him try what he can.
Encourage him with words and a helping hand.
Do not keep him sheltered from trying what he must.
You'll build his confidence, so in you, mom, he can trust.

More – See Page

20____ _____ _____

20____ _____ _____

20____ _____ _____

20____ _____ _____

20____ _____ _____

20____ _____ _____

God has said,
"Never will I leave you;
never will I forsake you."
So we say with confidence,
"The Lord is my helper;
I will not be afraid."
Hebrews 13:5b,6a

August 22

I remember a time before kids, when I checked everything off my "list".
I felt good, I was contented knowing there was nothing I had missed.
But now I often get frustrated, so little seems to get done.
My house is a mess, I'm tired all the time: life weighs on me like a ton.
Work also fills up my time, I just want to relax, have fun and enjoy.
Yet my children are my priority; they're my precious gifts, my lifelong joy.
Lord, help me be contented– not be thinking of all I need to do.
Let me show love, set reachable goals, and just keep focusing on You.

More – See Page

20___ _____ _____

20___ _____ _____

20___ _____ _____

20___ _____ _____

20___ _____ _____

20___ _____ _____

I have learned the secret of being content
in any and every situation, whether well fed or hungry,
whether living in plenty or in want.
I can do everything through Him who gives me strength.
Philippians 4:12b-13

August 23

There are instructions for most everything you buy.
There are directions, if they break and go awry.
But where's the manual for this child you've given me now?
Are The Bible and Your love, the guides to show me how?

More – See Page

20___ _____ _____

20___ _____ _____

20___ _____ _____

20___ _____ _____

20___ _____ _____

20___ _____ _____

All scripture is inspired by God
and is useful to teach us what is true
and make us realize what is wrong in our lives.
It corrects us when we are wrong
and teaches us to do what is right.
God uses it to prepare and equip his people to do good work.
2 Timothy 3:16,17 NLT

August 24

When my words do not seem to work or calm my child down,
When he's sad, and nothing brings smiles, I only see his frowns,
I stop what I'm doing, willing to get down on bended knee,
Then I reach out with love; he needs my touch and a hug from me.

More – See Page

20____ _____ _____
_____

20____ _____ _____
_____

20____ _____ _____
_____

20____ _____ _____
_____

20____ _____ _____
_____

20____ _____ _____
_____

Jesus reached out his hand
and touched the man.
"I am willing," he said.
Luke 5:13

August 25

Lord, give me insight to know my baby's needs,
Give me wisdom to know right and wrong.
Give me strength to make it through the day,
Give me a thankful heart all day long.

More – See Page

20___ _____ _____

_____

20___ _____ _____

_____

20___ _____ _____

_____

20___ _____ _____

_____

20___ _____ _____

_____

20___ _____ _____

_____

If any of you lacks wisdom, you should ask God,
who gives generously to all without finding fault,
and it will be given to you.
But when you ask, you must believe and not doubt,
because the one who doubts in like a wave on the sea,
blown and tossed by the wind.
James 1:5,6

August 26

I love our sweet, night-time ritual,
It started when my child was only a babe.
It has changed a bit throughout the years;
Stories, songs, books, discussing what he had made.
We end with a backrub and a prayer,
Then I tiptoe softly to the door.
Then I hear his little request:
"Please Mom, please, can I have just one more. . .?"
Just one more song, one story or drink,
One more trip to the potty tonight.
Are they real needs, or stalls, or wants?
Could a "no" bring tears, or start a fight?
Lord, please generously give me wisdom,
So each night I know how to reply.
Let him know I care, but be consistent,
Then I can leave with a smile, and a sigh.

More – See Page

20____ _____ _____

20____ _____ _____

20____ _____ _____

20____ _____ _____

20____ _____ _____

20____ _____ _____

For wisdom will enter your heart,
and knowledge will fill you with joy.
Wise choices will watch over you.
Understanding will keep you safe.
Proverbs 2:10-11 NLT

August 27

When Daddy is not home, whether at work or play,
I could talk about him in a negative way.
But I need to be positive in the words I say
So their love-bond will strengthen even when he's away.

More – See Page

20___ _____ _____

_____

20___ _____ _____

_____

20___ _____ _____

_____

20___ _____ _____

_____

20___ _____ _____

_____

20___ _____ _____

_____

"Let me give you a new command: Love one another.
In the same way I loved you, you love one another.
This is how everyone will recognize
that you are my disciples—
when they see the love you have for each other."
John 13:34,35 MSG

August 28

A summer sunset sky,
Of pink, purple, and blue
Reminds me . . .
Each day is a work of art
Created for me by You.

More – See Page

20___ _____ _____

20___ _____ _____

20___ _____ _____

20___ _____ _____

20___ _____ _____

20___ _____ _____

Lord, our Lord, how majestic
is Your name in all the earth!
You have set your glory in the heavens.
Psalm 8:1

August 29

My time at home is precious, I know that ever so well!
I love talking and playing with my child, but how often am I on my cell?
Computer time, phone time, seem to eat up the minutes each day.
I am always saying, "Just a minute!" when they ask me to come out and play.
Lord, help me be wise and learn to set boundaries and limits of my own.
Let my child feel my love, and not take second place to the
Internet or phone.

More – See Page

20___ _____ _____

_____

20___ _____ _____

_____

20___ _____ _____

_____

20___ _____ _____

_____

20___ _____ _____

_____

20___ _____ _____

_____

The instructions of the Lord are perfect, reviving the soul.
The decrees of the Lord are trustworthy, making wise the simple.
Psalm 19:7 NLT

August 30

I try to keep myself in shape;
I try to tune in to what is "cool."
Yet, now I've noticed something
That's not the exception, but the rule.
"Mom can I wear your shirt?"
"Your jeans fit me just fine."
My teen likes my taste and size,
But are my clothes hers or mine?

More – See Page

20___ _____ _____

20___ _____ _____

20___ _____ _____

20___ _____ _____

20___ _____ _____

20___ _____ _____

For the happy heart,
life is a continual feast.
Proverbs 15:15 NLT

August 31

I was asked to host a group of moms for dinner at my plain, simple house.
But it's so small. What will I cook? What if they see that pesky mouse?
There are so many others who are much better at this than me.
They make it look simple, Pintress®-perfect, such a delight to see!
But I promised I'd do anything for You, Lord, whatever You asked me to do.
Yet this is way out of my comfort zone! Not only that, what will I wear, too?
I need to stop fretting and pray, asking for your guidance from above.
Are you asking me to do this? Ok, now I feel your peace and love.
Yes, Lord, I will obey you and open my doors to all who come that night,
For fun and fellowship and I'll keep the food simple, delicious, and light.
I will invite my new friend to help me, who has different talents than me.
Please take this offering, multiply it, whether there are many or just three!

More – See Page

20____ _____ _____

20____ _____ _____

20____ _____ _____

20____ _____ _____

20____ _____ _____

20____ _____ _____

Taking the five loaves and the two fish and looking up to heaven,
he gave thanks and broke the loaves. They all ate and were satisfied,
and the disciples picked up twelve basketfuls
of broken pieces of bread and fish.
The number of men who had eaten was five thousand.
Mark 6:41a,42,43,44

September 1

But Mom,
Don't get depressed,
Thinking about getting older.
Think of it as one day closer
To living with Jesus
Where with Him
You will be young forever.

More – See Page

20____ _____ _____

_____

20____ _____ _____

_____

20____ _____ _____

_____

20____ _____ _____

_____

20____ _____ _____

_____

20____ _____ _____

_____

Gray hair is a crown of glory;
it is gained by living a godly life.
Proverbs 16:31 NLT

September 2

"Kick the ball!" "Get up!"
"No. . .run the OTHER way!"
Parents yell excitedly
On soccer's opening day.
My daughter falls and cries,
She got kicked hard in the knee.
A coach lovingly picks her up,
And carries her to me.

More – See Page

20___ _____ _____

20___ _____ _____

20___ _____ _____

20___ _____ _____

20___ _____ _____

20___ _____ _____

He heals the brokenhearted
and bandages their wounds.
Psalm 147:3 NLT

September 3

At "two," the ME in each one of us is at its peak,
MY wants, MY needs, is all a "two" wants to seek.
As we grow, and we're aware of others in our life,
The ME still appears, especially in times of strife.
But now as a mom, it's my child's needs I willingly meet.
God has replaced the big ME with His tender love so sweet.

More – See Page

20___ _____ _____

20___ _____ _____

20___ _____ _____

20___ _____ _____

20___ _____ _____

20___ _____ _____

Fulfill my joy by being like-minded, having the same love,
being of one accord, of one mind.
Let nothing be done through selfish ambition or conceit,
but in lowliness of mind let each esteem others better than himself.
Let each of you look out not only for his own interests,
but also for the interests of others.
Let this mind be in you which was also in Christ Jesus.
Philippians 2:2,3,4,5 NKJV

September 4

It was a typical trip to the grocery store
With my two little ones sitting in the cart.
We paid, and I was putting food in the car,
Pulled out my keys, preparing for the car to start.
That's when I saw it, under the cart basket.
Now in plain view as it could possibly be,
A gallon of white vinegar had escaped
Unnoticed by the checker as well as me.
No one would know if I ignored it,
And I just jumped into my car to go.
But You know, Lord, it would be stealing,
It was a clear and definite NO.
So, out of their car seats, back into the cart,
We wheeled back through the grocery store door.
Thank you, Lord, for another teachable moment,
One that was clear, and impossible to ignore.

More – See Page

20____ _____ _____

20____ _____ _____

20____ _____ _____

20____ _____ _____

20____ _____ _____

20____ _____ _____

So commit yourselves wholeheartedly to these words of mine.
Teach them to your children.
Talk about them when you are at home and when you are on the road,
when you are going to bed and when you are getting up.
Deuteronomy 11:18a,19 NLT

September 5

Letting go, letting your child try something
For the very first time is hard to do.
You could easily do it yourself and
Save some valuable time for both of you.
Yet he needs to try, he will probably take some spills,
Before he finally gets it right.
Encourage his effort, find the good,
Self-sufficiency–the long term goal to keep in sight.

More – See Page

20___ _____ _____
_____

20___ _____ _____
_____

20___ _____ _____
_____

20___ _____ _____
_____

20___ _____ _____
_____

20___ _____ _____
_____

The godly may trip seven times,
but they will get up again.
Proverbs 24:16a NLT

September 6

My children really have challenged my patience today.
My husband and I aren't expressing well what we say.
My aging parents are needing my attention more and more.
Lord, I need your help to renew my joy, and let my heart soar.
In no time at all, He answered my prayerful plea.
He reminded me He's in charge, it's not about me!
He whispered it's all about love and wants to enlarge my heart,
So I can serve with compassion and patience. . .Today I'll start!

More – See Page

20___ _____ _____
       _____

20___ _____ _____
       _____

20___ _____ _____
       _____

20___ _____ _____
       _____

20___ _____ _____
       _____

20___ _____ _____
       _____

May the Lord make your love increase
and overflow for each other
and for everyone else,
just as ours does for you.
1 Thessalonians 3:12

September 7

Pick out a Bible verse from the "breakfast bin"
Read it, say grace, it's a good way to begin.

More – See Page

20___ _____ _____

_____

20___ _____ _____

_____

20___ _____ _____

_____

20___ _____ _____

_____

20___ _____ _____

_____

20___ _____ _____

_____

Let the godly sing for joy to the Lord;
it is fitting for the pure to praise him.
For the word of the Lord holds true,
and we can trust everything he does.
He loves whatever is just and good;
the unfailing love of the Lord fills the earth.
Psalm 33:1,4,5 NLT

September 8

On your first day of school
As I walked you to the bus
You were excited and giggly,
You didn't want me to fuss.
As you climbed up the steps
You glanced back at me with fear,
So I smiled, blew you a kiss,
Turned and wiped away my tear.

More – See Page

20____ _____ _____
_____

20____ _____ _____
_____

20____ _____ _____
_____

20____ _____ _____
_____

20____ _____ _____
_____

20____ _____ _____
_____

Be strong and courageous.
Do not be afraid; do not be discouraged,
for the Lord your God will be with you
wherever you go.
Joshua 1:9

September 9

Just as I'm ready to make the bed,
My child jumps in and covers her head.
Now there is a big lump that moves, laughs, and giggles.
I might as well join her and hug out those wiggles.

More – See Page

20____ _____ _____

20____ _____ _____

20____ _____ _____

20____ _____ _____

20____ _____ _____

20____ _____ _____

A cheerful heart is good medicine,
but a broken spirit saps a person's strength.
Proverbs 17:22 NLT

September 10

The house is quiet. The bedrooms stay neat.
I'm making dinner for only two of us to eat.
There's college, jobs, or places of their own,
And I'm anxiously awaiting our talks on the phone.
But on the weekends and the holidays,
Guess who is at our front door
. . . Borrowing the car, looking in the Fridge,
Bags of laundry on the floor?

More – See Page

20___ _____ _____

20___ _____ _____

20___ _____ _____

20___ _____ _____

20___ _____ _____

20___ _____ _____

To everything there is a season,
a time for every purpose under heaven:
I know that nothing is better for them than to rejoice
and to do good in their lives, and also that every man
should eat and drink and enjoy the good
of all his labor- it is the gift of God.
Ecclesiastes 3:1,12,13 NKJV

September 11

My loved one is gone,
I'll never forget that day.
Yet others get busy,
And let it pass away.
Today is for memories.
Tomorrow I may mourn.
But I smile with thanksgiving,
Thinking of the day he was born.

More – See Page

20___ _____ _____
_____

20___ _____ _____
_____

20___ _____ _____
_____

20___ _____ _____
_____

20___ _____ _____
_____

20___ _____ _____
_____

Now when Jesus saw the crowds,
he went up on a mountainside and sat down.
His disciples came to him, and he began to teach them.
"Blessed are those who mourn,
for they will be comforted."
Matthew 5:1,2,4

September 12

Recycle your children's artwork;
Encourage them to do more.
The most meaningful card to their Grandma
May come off your refrigerator door.

More – See Page

20___   _____   _____

20___   _____   _____

20___   _____   _____

20___   _____   _____

20___   _____   _____

20___   _____   _____

A wise son brings joy to his father.
Proverbs 10:1a

September 13

Correcting homework
Or evaluating a job that's done,
First, find the good points
And praise each, one by one.
Then lovingly share
What needs improvement still,
Downplaying his mistakes,
Reaffirming his existing skills.

More – See Page

20____ _____ _____
        _____

20____ _____ _____
        _____

20____ _____ _____
        _____

20____ _____ _____
        _____

20____ _____ _____
        _____

20____ _____ _____
        _____

There has never been the slightest doubt in my mind
that the God who started this great work in you
would keep at it and bring it to a flourishing finish
on the very day Christ Jesus appears.
Philippians 1:6 MSG

September 14

I came up with a new plan.
It's totally changed our morning routine.
It is working well with our 5-year-old,
His older siblings, and even our pre-teen.
It's also helping us at bedtime,
And even when we go to the store.
Now my children aren't always asking me:
"Mommy please buy me this one thing more?"

. . . continued

More – See Page

20___ _____ _____
_____

20___ _____ _____
_____

20___ _____ _____
_____

20___ _____ _____
_____

20___ _____ _____
_____

20___ _____ _____
_____

From a wise mind comes wise speech;
the words of the wise are persuasive.
Proverbs 16:23 NLT

September 15

It's called the *Morning Motivator*,
They love checking-off each thing they daily do.
They are smiling and ready on time for school,
And rewarded for promptness and follow-through.
They each have three containers
To deposit their hard-earned money in.
Managing their funds for: fun, savings and God.
We've all decided this is a Win-Win!

More – See Page

20___ _____ _____

20___ _____ _____

20___ _____ _____

20___ _____ _____

20___ _____ _____

20___ _____ _____

"Should people cheat God? Yet, you have cheated me!
But, you ask, 'What do you mean? When did I cheat you?'
You have cheated me of the tithes and offerings due me.
Bring all the tithes into the store house so there will be enough food
in my Temple. If you do," says the Lord of Heaven's Armies,
"I will open the windows of heaven for you. I will pour out a blessing so great
you won't have enough room to take it in! Try it!"
Malachi 3:8,10 NLT

**Download your FREE Parenting Tool, "The Morning Motivator" at:
www.joyinparenting.com

September 16

A new school year, there's so much to do:
With forms, fundraisers, activities, too.
Yet, find the time to pray for each and every teacher.
Write a note of thanks; your love will surely reach her.

More – See Page

20___ _____ _____

_____

20___ _____ _____

_____

20___ _____ _____

_____

20___ _____ _____

_____

20___ _____ _____

_____

20___ _____ _____

_____

Dear brothers and sisters, pray for us!
1 Thessalonians 5:25 NLT

September 17

When I leave in the morning to be gone all day,
I picture you having fun at your school or play.
But no matter where I am, and whatever I do,
You're in my thoughts always, I truly love you!

More – See Page

20____ _____ _____

_____

20____ _____ _____

_____

20____ _____ _____

_____

20____ _____ _____

_____

20____ _____ _____

_____

20____ _____ _____

_____

Let love and faithfulness never leave you;
bind them around your neck,
write them on the tablet of your heart.
Proverbs 3:3

September 18

The first cute smile, the first real crawl.
The first new bike, the first bad fall.
A first can be fun, if it leaves no lasting scar,
But I'm still worried,
How about the first time our teen drives our car?!

More – See Page

20___ _____ _____

20___ _____ _____

20___ _____ _____

20___ _____ _____

20___ _____ _____

20___ _____ _____

Don't fret or worry. Instead of worrying, pray.
Let petitions and praises shape your worries into prayers,
letting God know your concerns.
Before you know it, a sense of God's wholeness,
everything coming together for good,
will come and settle you down.
It's wonderful what happens
when Christ displaces worry at the center of your life.
Philippians 4:6,7 MSG

September 19

A child remembers everything he hears and sees.
He memorizes stories, a new song's a breeze.
What else does he recall from a day with you. . .
Phone talk, your music, TV commercials, too?
Though an imprint on the sand may be washed away,
An imprint on a young mind may be there to stay.

More – See Page

20___ _____ _____

20___ _____ _____

20___ _____ _____

20___ _____ _____

20___ _____ _____

20___ _____ _____

Keep putting into practice all you learned and received from me—
everything you heard from me and saw me doing.
Then the God of peace will be with you.
Philippians 4:9 NLT

September 20

It is date night, so where do we go?
To Netflix © or find a favorite YouTube © show.
The evening is planned, we cannot wait,
Then our daughter wakes up sick from something she ate.
Our son cries since his sister is so sad,
So I cuddle our daughter, our son is with Dad.
Now it's after ten, do we start the show?
No! We're off to bed. Where did date night go?

More – See Page

20___ _____ _____

_____

20___ _____ _____

_____

20___ _____ _____

_____

20___ _____ _____

_____

20___ _____ _____

_____

20___ _____ _____

_____

Take tender care of those who are weak.
Be patient with everyone.
1 Thessalonians 5:14b NLT

September 21

If I want my child to be gentle, patient and kind;
Considerate of those he may reach,
I need to be an example daily and take the time,
To lovingly listen, guide, and teach.

More – See Page

20___ _____ _____

20___ _____ _____

20___ _____ _____

20___ _____ _____

20___ _____ _____

20___ _____ _____

Therefore I, a prisoner for serving the Lord,
beg you to lead a life worthy of your calling,
for you have been called by God.
Always be humble and gentle, be patient with each other,
making allowance for each other's faults because of your love.
Ephesians 4:1,2 NLT

September 22

Do I expect perfection from my children,
My husband, and even me?
Do I get upset when things aren't going 'my way'
And not turning out the way I want them to be?
Yet, often my words speak the opposite,
Saying "It's okay to make mistakes."
Lord, let me learn from my own words,
For myself, my husband's, and children's sake.

More – See Page

20___ _____ _____

20___ _____ _____

20___ _____ _____

20___ _____ _____

20___ _____ _____

20___ _____ _____

Let us think of ways to motivate one another
to acts of love and good works.
Hebrews 10:24 NLT

September 23

My young child asked me,
"What does God look like and do all day?
Is He bigger than our house?
Does He watch me when I sleep and play?"
Before I answered, I prayed,
To His Word, He directed me to read.
"The Son is the image of the invisible God."
It's about love and planting love seeds.
God the Father is a caring, kind healer
Who created us and sees you and me;
But He's also almighty and powerful,
Stronger than the wind and bigger than the sea.

. . .continued

More – See Page

20___ _____ _____

20___ _____ _____

20___ _____ _____

20___ _____ _____

20___ _____ _____

20___ _____ _____

Christ is the visible image of the invisible God.
He existed before anything was created
and is supreme over all creations,
for through him God created everything
in the heavenly realms and on earth.
Colossians 1:15,16a NLT

September 24

Jesus the Son said He was in the Father,
And the Father was in Him, too.
He said no one comes to the Father except through Him,
Ask Him, that's all you have to do.
My child may not understand
All my words that I shared with him today.
Often, it's hard for me to imagine God so mighty,
Yet caring about what I do and say.
Lord, take these words and use them
In my child's life and heart.
I pray I'm always open to Your words of truth,
Let this only be the start.

More – See Page

20___ _____ _____

_____

20___ _____ _____

_____

20___ _____ _____

_____

20___ _____ _____

_____

20___ _____ _____

_____

20___ _____ _____

_____

Jesus told him, "I am the way, the truth and the life.
No one can come to the Father except through me.
If you had really known me, you would know who my Father is.
From now on, you do know him and have seen him!
Just believe that I am in the Father and the Father is in me.
Or at least believe because of the work you have seen me do."
John 14:6,7,11 NLT

September 25

Cell phones are a reality and a blessing.
We use them every day.
But they can be a hinderance and addictive,
Influencing what my child might do and say.
I pray for wisdom and direction
On when to give my children their own cell.
I want them to be safe and to reach me,
No matter where I am or what they want to tell.
But, I realize, I too must be an example
When I use my computer or my phone.
Please guide and help me with this issue.
I rest in You! I'm so thankful I'm not alone.

More – See Page

20____ _____ _____

20____ _____ _____

20____ _____ _____

20____ _____ _____

20____ _____ _____

20____ _____ _____

For the Lord gives wisdom;
from his mouth come knowledge and understanding.
Proverbs 2:6

September 26

After having a baby I look in the mirror;
I see ripples, dimples, and layers, I fear.
My baby was worth it, no questioning that.
God used me for a miracle! It's all just "baby" fat.
Since it took nine months for my baby to grow,
I'll give myself the same for this weight to go!

More – See Page

20___ _____ _____

20___ _____ _____

20___ _____ _____

20___ _____ _____

20___ _____ _____

20___ _____ _____

Sing praises to God, sing praises;
sing praises to our King, sing praises!
Psalm 47: 6 NLT

September 27

No matter what grade
Your child receives on a test,
Make sure he knows
He is still your all-time best!

More – See Page

20___ _____ _____

20___ _____ _____

20___ _____ _____

20___ _____ _____

20___ _____ _____

20___ _____ _____

He comforts us in all our troubles
so that we can comfort others.
When they are troubled,
we will be able to give them
the same comfort God has given us.
2 Corinthians 1:4 NLT

September 28

Some people get excited about
Climbing a mountain,
Or sailing the open sea.
But seeing my son's face
As he rides his first bike
Is today's excitement for me.

More – See Page

20____ _____ _____

20____ _____ _____

20____ _____ _____

20____ _____ _____

20____ _____ _____

20____ _____ _____

May the Lord bless you and protect you.
May the Lord smile on you and be gracious to you.
May the Lord show you His favor
and give you His peace.
Numbers 6:24,25,26 NLT

September 29

Give him a hug. Say you're sorry.
Your brother is your best friend!
For in the future you will see,
On each other you will depend.

More – See Page

20___ _____ _____

20___ _____ _____

20___ _____ _____

20___ _____ _____

20___ _____ _____

20___ _____ _____

Therefore, if you are offering your gift at the altar
and there remember that your brother or sister
has something against you,
leave your gift there in front of the altar.
First go and be reconciled to them;
then come and offer your gift.
Matthew 5:23,24

September 30

"Mom, could you please pick me up from school today?"
"Mom, could you sew this rip in my uniform from yesterday?"
"Mom, can my friend come over for dinner tonight?"
"Mom, what should I do? My friend and I got into a fight!"

Today's one of those days. I need to stop everything and just pray,
Remembering, it's not an obligation, but a chance to serve in this way.
I need to show love, listen and reflect Jesus' servant's heart,
There's no time like right now to change my attitude and just start.

More – See Page

20___ _____ _____
      _____

20___ _____ _____
      _____

20___ _____ _____
      _____

20___ _____ _____
      _____

20___ _____ _____
      _____

20___ _____ _____
      _____

For even the Son of Man
did not come to be served,
but to serve,
and to give his life as a ransom for many.
Mark 10:45

October 1

Going the wrong way
On a one-way street could cause pain.
So follow God's one-way life signs
To be happy and remain sane.

More – See Page

20____ _____ _____

_____

20____ _____ _____

_____

20____ _____ _____

_____

20____ _____ _____

_____

20____ _____ _____

_____

20____ _____ _____

_____

Blessed are those who find wisdom,
those who gain understanding,
for she is more profitable than silver
and yields better returns than gold.
Her ways are pleasant ways, and all her paths are peace.
She is a tree of life to those who take hold of her;
those who hold her fast will be blessed.
Proverbs 3:13,14,17,18

October 2

At lunch when I can't be there
A cookie-cuttered cheese heart says,
"I love you and really care."

More – See Page

20___ _____ _____

20___ _____ _____

20___ _____ _____

20___ _____ _____

20___ _____ _____

20___ _____ _____

This is how God showed his love among us:
He sent his one and only Son into the world
that we might live through him.
This is love: not that we loved God,
but that he loved us
and sent his Son as an atoning sacrifice for our sins.
We love because he first loved us.
1 John 4:9,10,19

October 3

I have them captive: they're all buckled up.
Doors are locked: outsiders can't interrupt.
It's the perfect time while driving the van
To teach, to sing, and to listen to my clan.

More – See Page

20___ _____ _____

20___ _____ _____

20___ _____ _____

20___ _____ _____

20___ _____ _____

20___ _____ _____

Let the message about Christ,
in all its richness, fill your lives.
Teach and counsel each other with all the wisdom he gives.
Sing psalms and hymns and spiritual songs
to God with thankful hearts.
Colossians 3:16 NLT

October 4

There is one thing I want you to know,
It's that to strangers and even to friends,
It is okay to say NO!
Life is so fleeting; you are growing up so fast.
There are many who will want your time.
Be discerning, making special moments last.

More – See Page

20___ _____ _____

_____

20___ _____ _____

_____

20___ _____ _____

_____

20___ _____ _____

_____

20___ _____ _____

_____

20___ _____ _____

_____

Lord, remind me how brief my time on earth will be.
Remind me that my days are numbered—how fleeting life is.
You have made my life no longer than the width of my hand.
My entire lifetime is just a moment to you;
at best, each of us is but a breath.
And so, Lord, where do I put my hope?
My only hope is in you.
Psalm 39:4,5,7 NLT

October 5

With a tear of sadness, but more smiles of joy,
We took down the crib, our baby's a big boy.
Our big boy wants his own big boy bed,
New sheets and a pillow for his sweet head.
No more lifting him in or lifting him out,
Instead he wants to jump and shout!
No more crib bars and rails to keep him in,
Maybe he'll surprise me and for once sleep in.

More – See Page

20___ _____ _____

20___ _____ _____

20___ _____ _____

20___ _____ _____

20___ _____ _____

20___ _____ _____

May he give you the desire of your heart
and make all your plans succeed.
May we shout for joy over your victory
and lift up our banner in the name of our God.
Psalm 20:4,5

October 6

If I listen when she is young, and look her in the eye.
If I give her hugs and kisses, as each week flies by.
If I treat her with honesty, and teach her truths about You.
Then I'll be doing my best, the best that I can do.

More – See Page

20___ _____ _____

20___ _____ _____

20___ _____ _____

20___ _____ _____

20___ _____ _____

20___ _____ _____

Let each generation tell its children of your mighty acts;
let them proclaim your power.
I will meditate on your majestic, glorious splendor
and your wonderful miracles.
Psalm 145:4,5 NLT

October 7

It is just a normal morning, but I woke up grouchy today.
I'm not sure why, but I'm not acting in a kind and patient way.
The smallest things, even children's noises, make me almost mad.
They're just being children, yet I'm not being gentle, it's so sad.
Being a mom is one of my major callings, a dream and prayer come true.
To show love, gentleness, and patience—I need daily help from You!

More – See Page

20___ _____ _____
_____

20___ _____ _____
_____

20___ _____ _____
_____

20___ _____ _____
_____

20___ _____ _____
_____

20___ _____ _____
_____

As a prisoner for the Lord, then,
I urge you to live a life worthy of the calling you have received.
Be completely humble and gentle;
be patient, bearing with one another in love.
Ephesians 4:1,2

October 8

I have a drawer that's a total mess.
What's really in there is anyone's guess:
Pencils, thumb tacks, rubber bands, too,
Legos®, chewing gum, batteries, and glue.
To cleaning it all out, I am not opposed.
Yet, I'd rather forget it and keep it closed.

More – See Page

20___ _____ _____

20___ _____ _____

20___ _____ _____

20___ _____ _____

20___ _____ _____

20___ _____ _____

Therefore keep watch,
because you do not know on what day your Lord will come.
But understand this: If the owner of the house had known
at what time of night the thief was coming, he would have kept watch
and would not have let his house be broken into.
So you also must be ready,
because the Son of Man will come at an hour
when you do not expect him.
Matthew 24:42,43,44

October 9

I sat down with my older children today.
And told them they must listen to what I say.
No more threats from me or raising my voice,
I will ask once, to obey is their choice.
If they say "no", ignore me, or do not start to move,
There'll be consequences, or fun privileges removed.

More – See Page

20___ _____ _____
    _____

20___ _____ _____
    _____

20___ _____ _____
    _____

20___ _____ _____
    _____

20___ _____ _____
    _____

20___ _____ _____
    _____

Listen to your father, who gave you life,
And don't despise your mother when she is old.
The father of godly children has cause for joy.
What a pleasure to have children who are wise.
So give your father and mother joy!
May she who gave you birth be happy.
Proverbs 23:22,24,25 NLT

October 10

"I hate wasting good food," I always say.
So I save what's left and stash it away.
But what's behind that refrigerator door,
I do not mean to, but I tend to ignore.
Time passes by, then I finally pull out that dish:
"May I use that for science class?" is now my son's wish.

More – See Page

20___ _____ _____

_____

20___ _____ _____

_____

20___ _____ _____

_____

20___ _____ _____

_____

20___ _____ _____

_____

20___ _____ _____

_____

"No one lights a lamp and hides it in a clay jar
or puts it under a bed. Instead, they put it on a stand,
so that those who come in can see the light.
For there is nothing hidden that will not be disclosed,
and nothing concealed that will not be known
or brought out into the open."
Luke 8:16,17

October 11

I'm showered and dressed,
Ready to walk out the door.
You're fussy and crying,
You want me to hold you more.
Your nose is running, you're hot. . .
Why didn't I notice this before?
Lord, now what should I do?
Please open a new door.

More – See Page

20___ _____ _____
       _____

20___ _____ _____
       _____

20___ _____ _____
       _____

20___ _____ _____
       _____

20___ _____ _____
       _____

20___ _____ _____
       _____

God is our refuge and strength,
an ever-present help in trouble.
Psalm 46:1

October 12

When I was pregnant with our second baby,
We did something unexpected that prepared we three.
We shared a simple "family hug", arms entwined each day,
We all would kiss a "hole" in the "hug" as if to say,
There is always room for one more child for us to love.
All babies everywhere are a gift from God above!
For months on end, we would repeat this little act,
So our oldest child was used to this simple fact.
A little brother or sister would be loved by all,
Becoming best friends whether a child or grown tall.
Sure enough, as we carried our newborn through the door,
Our excited daughter came running to us, asking for more. . .
"More Family Hugs, and for real this time!" she joyfully said.
Lifting her up, smiling, she kept kissing his little head.
Now years later, I look back at that special birth day,
Thank you, Lord, they ARE best friends, which hopefully they'll stay!

More – See Page

20___ _____ _____

_____

20___ _____ _____

_____

20___ _____ _____

_____

20___ _____ _____

_____

20___ _____ _____

_____

20___ _____ _____

_____

Most important of all,
continue to show deep love for each other,
for love covers a multitude of sins.
1 Peter 4:8 NLT

October 13

Wash your hands with soap until they are clean.
Cover your mouth, then cough; there are germs unseen.
A mother is a teacher, a nurse, a friend;
A child learns from her, and on her he depends.

More – See Page

20____ _____ _____
_____

20____ _____ _____
_____

20____ _____ _____
_____

20____ _____ _____
_____

20____ _____ _____
_____

20____ _____ _____
_____

In the same way,
let your good deeds shine out for all to see,
so that everyone will praise your heavenly Father.
Matthew 5:16 NLT

October 14

My doctor tells me to exercise more,
Like jogging, swimming, or jumping a rope to skip.
But shouldn't he count my running the stairs,
With a child and laundry basket on my hip?

More – See Page

20____ _____ _____
        _____

20____ _____ _____
        _____

20____ _____ _____
        _____

20____ _____ _____
        _____

20____ _____ _____
        _____

20____ _____ _____
        _____

No discipline seems pleasant at the time, but painful.
Later on, however, it produces a harvest of righteousness
and peace for those who have been trained by it.
Hebrews 12:11

October 15

It's okay you made a mistake,
Mommy goofs up often, too.
Just try again, do your best,
That's all I will ask of you.

More – See Page

20___ _____ _____

20___ _____ _____

20___ _____ _____

20___ _____ _____

20___ _____ _____

20___ _____ _____

My dear children,
I write this to you so that you will not sin. But if anybody does sin,
we have an advocate with the Father—Jesus Christ, the Righteous One.
He is the atoning sacrifice for our sins,
and not only for ours
but also for the sins of the whole world.
1 John 2:1,2

October 16

Control over your child should decrease,
As their age and understanding increases.

More – See Page

20___ _____ _____

20___ _____ _____

20___ _____ _____

20___ _____ _____

20___ _____ _____

20___ _____ _____

Even a child is known by his actions,
by whether his conduct is pure and right.
Proverbs 20:11

October 17

My "two" is going through "It's MINE!", a typical childhood stage,
Not wanting to share; it's "Me", "My", "No"– I know it's just her age.
Yet, what is my excuse, when I too do not want to share?
I have so much. I need to give thanks. Show others I care.
Lord, help me to share cheerfully, I need to let go and gladly give away.
Let me be a model for my child, for You provide generously each day.

More – See Page

20___ _____ _____

_____

20___ _____ _____

_____

20___ _____ _____

_____

20___ _____ _____

_____

20___ _____ _____

_____

20___ _____ _____

_____

Each of you should give what you have decided in your heart to give,
not reluctantly or under compulsion, for God loves a cheerful giver.
And God is able to bless you abundantly,
so that in all things at all times, having all that you need,
you will abound in every good work.
2 Corinthians 9:7,8

October 18

I love you too much to let you act this way.
I care for you too much to see a day thrown away.
Because of my love, I'll teach you right and wrong.
No matter what you do, this love is ever strong.

More – See Page

20____ _____ _____

20____ _____ _____

20____ _____ _____

20____ _____ _____

20____ _____ _____

20____ _____ _____

My child, don't reject the Lord's discipline,
and don't be upset when he corrects you.
For the Lord corrects those he loves,
just as a father corrects a child in whom he delights.
Proverbs 3:11,12 NLT

October 19

The sink backs up, the toilet overflows,
The washer breaks, my old car needs a tow.
Once-in-awhile trials that give me a frown
Happen most often when my honey's out of town!

More – See Page

20___ _____ _____

_____

20___ _____ _____

_____

20___ _____ _____

_____

20___ _____ _____

_____

20___ _____ _____

_____

20___ _____ _____

_____

Cast your cares on the Lord and he will sustain you;
he will never let the righteous be shaken.
Psalm 55:22

October 20

Square roots, circumference, you ask me to clarify.
Atoms and molecules, what temperatures solids liquify?
Helping you with school lessons is a challenge each night.
I want to encourage and guide, but your homework I won't write.

More – See Page

20___ _____ _____

20___ _____ _____

20___ _____ _____

20___ _____ _____

20___ _____ _____

20___ _____ _____

Let the wise listen and add to their learning,
and let the discerning get guidance.
The fear of the Lord is the beginning of knowledge,
but fools despise wisdom and instruction.
Proverbs 1:5,7

October 21

You can't wait 'til they crawl, but then. . .watch out!
You can't wait 'til they talk, but then. . .they shout!
You can't wait 'til they're grown, but then. . .they're off on their own!
You can't wait for grandkids of your very own.
But don't wait for tomorrow! Enjoy today!
Savor each moment. It's more fun that way.

More – See Page

20____ _____ _____

_____

20____ _____ _____

_____

20____ _____ _____

_____

20____ _____ _____

_____

20____ _____ _____

_____

20____ _____ _____

_____

This is the day the Lord has made;
we will rejoice and be glad in it.
Psalm 118:24 NKJV

October 22

Lord, sharpen my mind so I can see
The things that hurt You from my child and me.
Lord soften my heart so I can feel
Your love for me and know it is real.

More – See Page

20____ _____ _____

20____ _____ _____

20____ _____ _____

20____ _____ _____

20____ _____ _____

20____ _____ _____

Search me, God, and know my heart;
test me and know my anxious thoughts.
Point out anything in me that offends you,
and lead me along the path of everlasting life.
Psalm 139:23,24 NLT

October 23

When your child has had a very tough day,
Get off the phone and turn your friends away.
Find a place to listen for just you two,
And eye-to-eye, let him share it with you.

More – See Page

20___ _____ _____

20___ _____ _____

20___ _____ _____

20___ _____ _____

20___ _____ _____

20___ _____ _____

This is what the Lord Almighty said:
"Administer true justice;
show mercy and compassion to one another. "
Zechariah 7:9

October 24

My child is dreaming about what he plans to do or be.
He has many gifts and talents, that is so plain to see.
I want to encourage and cheer on all these dreams and hopes,
Be there when he stumbles, help him up, and teach him to cope.
But I also want to remind him, it is You who has the final "say,"
To be prayerfully open for new thoughts, it is You directing his days.

More – See Page

20____ _____ _____

20____ _____ _____

20____ _____ _____

20____ _____ _____

20____ _____ _____

20____ _____ _____

We can make our plans,
but the Lord determines our steps.
Proverbs 16:9 NLT

October 25

Let your child be a child,
Finding joy in simple things.
Let him be silly, light and funny;
Let his voice freely sing!

More – See Page

20____ _____ _____

20____ _____ _____

20____ _____ _____

20____ _____ _____

20____ _____ _____

20____ _____ _____

He will fill your mouth with laughter
and your lips with shouts of joy.
Job 8:21

October 26

Just ask your child
If a freshly raked pile
Of crisp, crunchy, colorful fall leaves
Is recyclable?
He jumps in the pile,
is his reply.
Then stop what you are doing
And jump in with him!

More – See Page

20___ _____ _____

_____

20___ _____ _____

_____

20___ _____ _____

_____

20___ _____ _____

_____

20___ _____ _____

_____

20___ _____ _____

_____

He has made everything beautiful in its time.
He has also set eternity in the human heart;
yet no one can fathom what God has done from beginning to end.
Ecclesiastes 3:11

October 27

In the beginning, you're awake at night,
Rocking, feeding and humming one song more.
Much later, you're awake in the moonlight,
Just waiting for your teen's key in the door.

More – See Page

20____ _____ _____

20____ _____ _____

20____ _____ _____

20____ _____ _____

20____ _____ _____

20____ _____ _____

For the Lord is good and his love endures forever;
his faithfulness continues through all generations.
Psalm 100:5

October 28

Especially on weekends, there's one thing that's true.
As our children wake up, there's one thing they do.
It's as if a magnet is pulling each child
To our bed and bedroom; it gets sort of wild.
There's cuddling and hugging and rubbing of backs,
There's wiggling and giggling and tickling attacks.
But when it's all over, they scatter like mice,
Leaving a bed of destruction, yet the silence is nice.

More – See Page

20____ _____ _____

20____ _____ _____

20____ _____ _____

20____ _____ _____

20____ _____ _____

20____ _____ _____

By the seventh day God had finished the work
he had been doing;
so on the seventh day he rested from all his work.
Genesis 2:2

October 29

My busy toddler pulled down my purse today;
The insides are scattered on the floor in disarray.
I could get mad, not finding the humor in this first-time play;
Or I could teach, let her touch, and let her learn from it today.

More – See Page

20____ _____ _____

_____

20____ _____ _____

_____

20____ _____ _____

_____

20____ _____ _____

_____

20____ _____ _____

_____

20____ _____ _____

_____

She speaks with wisdom,
and faithful instruction is on her tongue.
Proverbs 31:26

October 30

Like a guardrail on a mountain road
Lessens a driver's fears,
Fair rules and limits set with love
Can prevent needless tears.

More – See Page

20____ _____ _____

20____ _____ _____

20____ _____ _____

20____ _____ _____

20____ _____ _____

20____ _____ _____

A gentle answer turns away wrath,
but a harsh word stirs up anger.
Proverbs 15:1

October 31

My child talked back to me today.
She did not obey or respect what I had to say.
Other moms tell me it is part of how they learn and grow,
Setting their own rules by deciding when to say Yes or No.
But I disagree, and immediately followed through.
You don't say NO to mom, or break God's rule that's true.
It is the only Commandment of the Ten with a promise to our child,
That by honoring us, she'll have a long full life, nothing crazy or wild.

More – See Page

20____ _____ _____

20____ _____ _____

20____ _____ _____

20____ _____ _____

20____ _____ _____

20____ _____ _____

Honor your father and mother.
Then you will live a long, full life
in the land the Lord your God is giving you.
Exodus 20:12 NLT

November 1

There comes a time
When every mom has to say "no,"
To protect and direct her children
In the way they should go.
Eight sides of a **Stop Sign**
Are a good tool to teach
The why's and when's to say "no;"
Their conscience to reach.

. . .continued

More – See Page

20___ _____ _____

_____

20___ _____ _____

_____

20___ _____ _____

_____

20___ _____ _____

_____

20___ _____ _____

_____

20___ _____ _____

_____

Direct your children onto the right path,
and when they are older, they will not leave it.
Proverbs 22:6 NLT

November 2

NOT OLD ENOUGH. . .

To handle responsibility—
Whether they're two or a new teen.
I give options, and my reasons
So they understand what I mean.

UNHEALTHY. . .

To their bodies—
Maybe their minds too.
Their bodies are a gift
And can't be fixed with Elmer's Glue ®.

. . .continued

More – See Page

20___ _____ _____

20___ _____ _____

20___ _____ _____

20___ _____ _____

20___ _____ _____

20___ _____ _____

When I was a child, I spoke as a child,
I understood as a child, I thought as a child;
but when I became a man, I put away childish things.
1 Corinthians 13:11 NKJV

My child, if sinners entice you, turn your back on them!
Proverbs 1:10 NLT

November 3

CAN'T AFFORD IT. . .

Even though all their friends
May own one today.
They might work and earn it,
It will be more appreciated that way.

ILLEGAL. . .

Means a definite "no"
From me and our country's laws.
There are no "ifs" or "maybes",
But I do explain the "because."

. . .continued

More – See Page

20___ _____ _____
_____

20___ _____ _____
_____

20___ _____ _____
_____

20___ _____ _____
_____

20___ _____ _____
_____

20___ _____ _____
_____

No one can serve two masters. . .
you cannot serve both God and money.
Matthew 6:24

Remind the believers to submit to the government and its officers.
They should be obedient, always ready to do what is good.
Titus 3:1 NLT

November 4

INCONSIDERATE. . .

Of someone's feelings,
Property, or even privacy.
Ask, "How would I feel
If someone did this to me?"

DISHONEST. . .

By their actions, words,
Or even silence too.
I need to trust and believe
That everything they say is true.

. . .continued

More – See Page

20___ _____ _____

20___ _____ _____

20___ _____ _____

20___ _____ _____

20___ _____ _____

20___ _____ _____

Do to others whatever you would like them to do to you.
This is the essence of all that is taught in the law and the prophets.
Matthew 7:12 NLT

The Lord detests lying lips, but he delights in those who tell the truth.
Proverbs 12:22 NLT

November 5

NOT ENOUGH TIME. . .

If often a real answer
To give them today.
But if the request is worthy,
Find time another day.

UNSAFE. . .

To themselves or
To others it may hurt.
Help them always be aware
And on "accident alert."

. . .continued

More – See Page

20___ _____ _____
     _____

20___ _____ _____
     _____

20___ _____ _____
     _____

20___ _____ _____
     _____

20___ _____ _____
     _____

20___ _____ _____
     _____

Those who are wise will find a time and a way to do what is right,
for there is a time and a way for everything,
even when a person is in trouble.
Ecclesiastes 8:5b,6 NLT

But whoever listens to me will live in safety
and be at ease, without fear of harm.
Proverbs 1:33

November 6

Help them memorize each side,
So eight reasons they will know
When to say to themselves and to others,
"Stop," "I won't," and "It's Definitely NO!"

More – See Page

20____ _____ _____

20____ _____ _____

20____ _____ _____

20____ _____ _____

20____ _____ _____

20____ _____ _____

My son, keep your father's command
and do no forsake your mother's teaching.
Proverbs 6:20

**Download your FREE Parenting Tool, "The Stop Sign"
at: www.joyinparenting.com

November 7

I have heard it said:
"Prepare the child for the road, not the road for the child."
Am I protecting my children way too much?
Am I afraid of what they may do, see and touch?
Am I fixing things so they won't ever get hurt,
Emotionally, physically, like even falling in the dirt?
I need to re-think this and make sure they're ready to go
To face the world with Your truths and commands they know.
I need to teach them to remember the deeds you have done,
Your wonders, Your grace, Your love for everyone.
I need to let go more, trust You, and let You lead.
And buy them a children's Bible they *want* to read.
That's how I will prepare them for the future road,
Already I feel lightened from my heavy 'mommy load.'

More – See Page

20____ _____ _____

20____ _____ _____

20____ _____ _____

20____ _____ _____

20____ _____ _____

20____ _____ _____

We will tell the next generation the praiseworthy deeds of the Lord,
his power, and the wonders he has done.
So the next generation would know them, even the children yet to be born,
and they in turn would tell their children.
Psalms 78:4b,6

November 8

We're going on a date tonight!
It's nice to get dressed up and wear make-up, too!
The sitter has finally arrived
And a spritz of perfume is the last I do.
Even before I kissed my kids goodbye,
My eldest said, "Mommy, you smell so great!"
The fragrance of my perfume had reached her
Before I even said, "We won't be too late."
Then I pondered: Am I spreading the fragrance of Christ?
Do my family, my friends and others see You in all I say and do?
Are my actions, expressions, and my words like a sweet perfume?
I want my life to be an aroma of Christ, rising up to You!

More – See Page

20___ _____ _____
_____

20___ _____ _____
_____

20___ _____ _____
_____

20___ _____ _____
_____

20___ _____ _____
_____

20___ _____ _____
_____

Now he uses us to spread the knowledge of Christ
everywhere like a sweet perfume.
Our lives are a Christ-like fragrance rising up to God.
2 Corinthians 2:14b,15a NLT

November 9

Tiny tiptoes turn down the hall,
Many muffled giggles shared by all.
Seven slightly sleepy girls say,
"Can we sleep over again someday?"

More – See Page

20____ _____ _____

20____ _____ _____

20____ _____ _____

20____ _____ _____

20____ _____ _____

20____ _____ _____

Enter his gates with thanksgiving
and his courts with praise;
give thanks to him and praise his name.
Psalm 100:4

November 10

Saying "no" to a good friend
Is hard for my child to do,
When they get into mischief
Or want to try something new.
I must work to develop his conscience
So he can make good decisions alone.
Please give me wisdom and direction
To guide your gift given to me on loan.

More – See Page

20____ _____ _____

_____

20____ _____ _____

_____

20____ _____ _____

_____

20____ _____ _____

_____

20____ _____ _____

_____

20____ _____ _____

_____

Oh, the joys of those who do not follow the advice of the wicked,
or stand around with sinners, or join in with mockers.
But they delight in the law of the Lord,
meditating on it day and night.
Psalm 1:1,2 NLT

November 11

If we spent as much time teaching our children
To communicate and to resolve conflicts with love,
As we do letting them watch violent TV, games and movies
Or fighting with sticks, swords, guns, and gloves;
Then we might see gentle peace and discussions instead of wars.
But it's the mothers of our future soldiers
Who must first teach and open these new doors.

More – See Page

20____ _____ _____

20____ _____ _____

20____ _____ _____

20____ _____ _____

20____ _____ _____

20____ _____ _____

"You must love the Lord your God with all your heart,
all your soul, and all your mind.
This is the first and greatest commandment.
A second is equally important: Love your neighbor as yourself.
The entire law and all the demands of the prophets
are based on these two commandments."
Matthew 22:37-40 NLT

November 12

I might disagree with what my husband might say;
I might handle it differently if I did it my way.
But we must support each other and stand strong as one,
Learning, forgiving, and growing. . .or we will be overrun.

More – See Page

20____ _____ _____

_____

20____ _____ _____

_____

20____ _____ _____

_____

20____ _____ _____

_____

20____ _____ _____

_____

20____ _____ _____

_____

Let the peace of Christ rule in your heats,
since as members of one body
You were called to peace. And be thankful.
Colossians 3:15

November 13

Read to them when they're young
Read with them when they're old,
And they will read forever
Without being told.

More – See Page

20___ _____ _____

_____

20___ _____ _____

_____

20___ _____ _____

_____

20___ _____ _____

_____

20___ _____ _____

_____

20___ _____ _____

_____

You have been taught the holy Scriptures
from childhood, and they have given you the wisdom
to receive the salvation that comes by trusting in Christ Jesus.
2 Timothy 3:15 NLT

November 14

The magazines, blogs, and ads say,
"Dress for Success."
For a mother of a baby,
Success is when her top has no burp or nursing stains,
All of its buttons, and her hair looks a little better
Than when she got up in the morning.

More – See Page

20____ _____ _____

20____ _____ _____

20____ _____ _____

20____ _____ _____

20____ _____ _____

20____ _____ _____

From his abundance we have all received
one gracious blessing after another.
John 1:16 NLT

November 15

Your teacher called me today and told me something you did.
It makes me feel sad and confused, for it's something we forbid.
But first, let me hear your side; tell me honestly about your day.
I will listen and try to be fair, for I love you in every way.

More – See Page

20____ _____ _____

20____ _____ _____

20____ _____ _____

20____ _____ _____

20____ _____ _____

20____ _____ _____

Teach me, Lord, the way of your decrees,
that I may follow it to the end.
Give me understanding, so that I may keep your law
and obey it with all my heart.
Direct me in the path of your commands,
for there I find delight.
Psalm 119:33-35

November 16

"Touch it just once," I always say,
As I teach my child to put things away.
"Let it not find a place to rest,
Until you have found the place that is best."

More – See Page

20___ _____ _____

20___ _____ _____

20___ _____ _____

20___ _____ _____

20___ _____ _____

20___ _____ _____

A house is built by wisdom
and becomes strong through good sense.
Proverbs 24:3 NLT

November 17

The alarm rings. . .I think about my day.
It's cold and dark, in bed I'd rather stay.
But duty calls, yet it is quiet for a change;
I will take this time to pray. . .
For I know my outlook, He'll rearrange.

More – See Page

20____ _____ _____
        _____

20____ _____ _____
        _____

20____ _____ _____
        _____

20____ _____ _____
        _____

20____ _____ _____
        _____

20____ _____ _____
        _____

Do you not know? Have you not heard?
The Lord is the everlasting God,
the Creator of the ends of the earth.
He will not grow tired or weary,
and his understanding no one can fathom.
He gives strength to the weary
and increases the power of the weak.
Isaiah 40:28,29

November 18

My baby's now a pre-teen! Yikes!
Where did the precious time go?
Now with hormones, new friends, peer pressure. . .
What do I want her to know?

She is worthy!

She was designed with a purpose and a plan.
Every intricate little parts of her body
Were knitted together by God's own loving hand.

She is special!

No one is designed exactly like her.
She has talents, gifts, and abilities
That did not just accidently occur.

. . .continued

More – See Page

20___ _____ _____

20___ _____ _____

20___ _____ _____

20___ _____ _____

20___ _____ _____

20___ _____ _____

You made all the delicate, inner parts of my body
and knit me together in my mother's womb.
You saw me before I was born.
Every day of my life was recorded in your book.
Every moment was laid out before a single day had passed.
Psalm 139:13,16 NLT

November 19

She is loved!

There is nothing she could do to take my love away.
We might disagree, there may be firm limits,
But my love is constant, and forever here to stay!
I look forward to our special meals,
Shopping and our bedtime prayers and talks;
But maybe in the future, we'll connect better
Through texts, workouts, or taking long walks.
With Your help, I will do whatever it takes
To let her know I'm always on her side,
Not hovering, but listening—reminding her,
It's in You, Lord, we both need to abide.

More – See Page

20____ _____ _____

20____ _____ _____

20____ _____ _____

20____ _____ _____

20____ _____ _____

20____ _____ _____

Don't let anyone look down on you because you are young,
but set an example for the believers in speech,
in conduct, in love, in faith and in purity.
1 Timothy 4:12

November 20

Like my child, I'm learning to say "No"
To committees and functions and place to go.
Time is precious, our children are growing up so fast.
I want to savor it all and make each moment last.

More – See Page

20___ _____ _____

20___ _____ _____

20___ _____ _____

20___ _____ _____

20___ _____ _____

20___ _____ _____

There is a time for everything,
and a season for every activity under the heavens.
Ecclesiastes 3:1

November 21

Family night. . .What should we do?
Family night. . .Try something new.
Family night. . .No phones to ring.
Family night. . .A new song to sing.
Family night. . .Together having fun,
Ending with praises for God's only Son!

More – See Page

20___ _____ _____

20___ _____ _____

20___ _____ _____

20___ _____ _____

20___ _____ _____

20___ _____ _____

Sing to the Lord a new song;
sing to the Lord, all the earth.
Sing to the Lord, praise his name;
proclaim his salvation day after day.
Psalm 96:1,2

November 22

That is too bad you lost today,
But say, "Good job!" to your sister who won.
Next time you may be the winner,
So practice together and have some fun.

More – See Page

20___ _____ _____

20___ _____ _____

20___ _____ _____

20___ _____ _____

20___ _____ _____

20___ _____ _____

May the God who gives you endurance
and encouragement give you the same attitude
of mind toward each other that Christ Jesus had.
Romans 15:5

November 23

Family traditions are important,
It is the string in family ties.
Start a new tradition—
Let the kids make the pumpkin pies.

More – See Page

20____ _____ _____

20____ _____ _____

20____ _____ _____

20____ _____ _____

20____ _____ _____

20____ _____ _____

The Lord has done great things for us,
and we are filled with joy.
Psalm 126:3

November 24

You kneel by your child's bed to thank God for the day,
But your daughter is wound up from a busy day at play.
Take a moment to hug her, cuddle her, and help her feel calm.
Begin in a different way; say a prayer, and sing a psalm.

More – See Page

20___

20___

20___

20___

20___

20___

And he said: "Truly I tell you, unless you change
and become like little children,
you will never enter the kingdom of heaven.
Therefore, whoever takes the lowly position of this child
is the greatest in the kingdom of heaven.
And whoever welcomes one such child in my name welcomes me.
Matthew 18:3-5

November 25

As children pass from child to adult,
The problems of teen years seem to be our fault.
Release your child to God above,
Then feel His peace, His direction, and His love.

More – See Page

20____ _____ _____

20____ _____ _____

20____ _____ _____

20____ _____ _____

20____ _____ _____

20____ _____ _____

He tends his flock like a shepherd:
He gathers the lambs in his arms
and carries them close to his heart;
he gently leads those that have young.
Isaiah 40:11

November 26

I took my children on a little outing today,
It wasn't to a museum, or playground for them to play.
We instead visited a special home where the elderly live,
To talk with them, sing songs, and our homemade goodies to give.
These simple 'love gifts', brought many warm smiles and such joy,
My children beamed so bright, better than from a new-found toy!

More – See Page

20___ _____ _____
_____

20___ _____ _____
_____

20___ _____ _____
_____

20___ _____ _____
_____

20___ _____ _____
_____

20___ _____ _____
_____

Stand up in the presence of the elderly,
and show respect for the aged.
Fear your God. I am the Lord.
Leviticus 19:32 NLT

November 27

Usually we can overlook our children's faults.
Why can't we do the same for our husband's?

More – See Page

20___ _____ _____

_____

20___ _____ _____

_____

20___ _____ _____

_____

20___ _____ _____

_____

20___ _____ _____

_____

20___ _____ _____

_____

Bear with each other and forgive one another
if any of you has a grievance against someone.
Forgive as the Lord forgave you.
Colossians 3:13

November 28

I got hurt today; can't play games with you,
Like running, jumping, and hopscotch, too.
But give me a board game, and I'll show you my stuff;
Beating me at that will be sort of tough.
I might not be able to pick you up,
Or chase you around like a frisky pup.
But you can sit on my lap as I read and sing
The stories about Jesus, our Savior and King.

More – See Page

20___ _____ _____

20___ _____ _____

20___ _____ _____

20___ _____ _____

20___ _____ _____

20___ _____ _____

Come, my children, listen to me;
I will teach you the fear of the Lord.
Psalm 34:11

November 29

I remind my children to say "Thank You,"
And I try to do the same each day.
We tend to thank family, friends, and others,
But do I thank You in all I do and say?
So I want to thank You Lord, for WHO You are,
Not just for WHAT You always do.
You are Mighty, Loving, Unchanging –
My Savior, You will always be You!
I want to sing a song of joy
And shout out Your Holy name. . .
You're my Father, my Rock, my Provider,
I'll teach my children to do the same.
Help me not let a day go by,
In my busyness from morning to night,
Without taking a moment to Thank You.
Lord, it is YOU in whom I delight!

More – See Page

20____ _____ _____

_____

20____ _____ _____

_____

20____ _____ _____

_____

20____ _____ _____

_____

20____ _____ _____

_____

20____ _____ _____

_____

Come let us sing for joy to the Lord; let us shout aloud
to the Rock of our salvation. Let us come before him with thanksgiving
and extol him with music and song. For the Lord is the great God,
the great King above all gods.
Psalm 95:1,2,3

November 30

Teach your young children to first obey,
Then let them ask the "whys" to what you may say.
For keeping them safe is your first concern;
Now they're too young to decide and discern.

More – See Page

20____ _____ _____

20____ _____ _____

20____ _____ _____

20____ _____ _____

20____ _____ _____

20____ _____ _____

For I too was a son to my father,
still tender, and cherished by my mother.
Then he taught me, and he said to me,
"Take hold of my words with all your heart;
keep my commands, and you will live."
Proverbs 4:3,4

December 1

Something curious is happening, I'd like to know the reason.
Strangers stop to pat me as if tummies are "open season."
Now don't get me wrong, I truly love hugs and kisses.
I'm just trying to figure out exactly what this is.
It sort of tickles, but it seems odd and strange to me,
People who would pass me by, now want to touch and see.
But I am sure my baby must be feeling their love
While he is being created by our God above.
So I will just smile, listen, and gladly share my joy.
It's so exciting waiting for my little baby girl or boy.

More – See Page

20____ _____ _____

_____

20____ _____ _____

_____

20____ _____ _____

_____

20____ _____ _____

_____

20____ _____ _____

_____

20____ _____ _____

_____

But forget all that—
it is nothing compared to what I am going to do.
For I am about to do something new.
See, I have already begun! Do you not see it?
Isaiah 43:18,19 NLT

December 2

Starting a new Christmas tradition this year is easy.
Remembering to do it again next year is what's hard.

More – See Page

20____ _____ _____

20____ _____ _____

20____ _____ _____

20____ _____ _____

20____ _____ _____

20____ _____ _____

You can make many plans,
but the Lord's purpose will prevail.
Proverbs 19:21 NLT

December 3

It was a cold school morning, yet, all my three had eaten.
Their back-packs ready, and they even had combed their hair.
So I said, "Jump in the car! A special surprise!
Since you all are ready, we have some time to spare."
So off we drove to our most favorite coffee shop,
For three hot chocolates, and coffee for me 'to go'.
While waiting in the 'drive thru lane', I said:
"Let's give a gift to someone we don't know!"

. . .continued

More – See Page

20___ _____ _____

20___ _____ _____

20___ _____ _____

20___ _____ _____

20___ _____ _____

20___ _____ _____

And do not forget to do good
and share with others,
for with such sacrifices God is pleased.
Hebrews 13:16

December 4

I drove up to pay for our drinks, then said:
"Here's money to pay for the car behind us too."
There was a couple in an old car waiting,
They had no idea what we were going to do.
As they pulled up to the cashier's window,
We could see the smiles our gift gave that day.
But I especially loved the joy and laughter
From my children as we gave this gift away.
It was a very simple act of sharing,
With an elderly couple cold and on the go.
But to serve others, we serve Jesus,
That's what I want my children to learn and know!

More – See Page

20____ _____ _____

_____

20____ _____ _____

_____

20____ _____ _____

_____

20____ _____ _____

_____

20____ _____ _____

_____

20____ _____ _____

_____

"The King will reply,
'Truly I tell you, whatever you did for one of the least
of these brothers and sisters of mine, you did for me.'"
Matthew 25:40

December 5

Am I much more interested
In completing my lists today,
Than being kind and loving
In all things I do and say?

More – See Page

20___ _____ _____

20___ _____ _____

20___ _____ _____

20___ _____ _____

20___ _____ _____

20___ _____ _____

Jesus replied, "The most important commandment is this:
'Listen, O Israel! The Lord our God, the Lord is the one and only Lord.
And you must love the Lord your God with all your heart,
all your soul, all your mind, and all your strength.'
The second is equally important:
'Love your neighbor as yourself.'
No other commandment is greater than these."
Mark 12:29,30,31 NLT

December 6

Look through Jesus' eyes
At your precious girl or boy.
Feel His love, His compassion,
His forgiveness and His joy!

More – See Page

20___ _____ _____

20___ _____ _____

20___ _____ _____

20___ _____ _____

20___ _____ _____

20___ _____ _____

The Lord your God in your midst,
The Mighty One, will save;
He will rejoice over you with gladness,
He will quiet you with His love,
He will rejoice over you with singing.
Zephaniah 3:17 NKJV

December 7

When I'm in a rush to get out the door,
My child wants to play with just one toy more.
I say, "Hurry!" yet she seems to go slow.
Yet it's not really on purpose, I know.
I need to get up earlier, plan better each day,
So there is time for surprises that get in the way.
I need to give notice before I say, "Let's Go!"
Then she will be ready with her smile all aglow.

More – See Page

20___ _____ _____
     _____

20___ _____ _____
     _____

20___ _____ _____
     _____

20___ _____ _____
     _____

20___ _____ _____
     _____

20___ _____ _____
     _____

In everything we do, we show we are true ministers of God.
We prove ourselves by our purity our understanding, our patience,
our kindness, by the Holy Spirit within us, and by our sincere love.
2 Corinthians 6:4a,6

December 8

My primary purpose at Christmas time is not
To buy presents, decorate the house, and send cards.
My purpose and responsibility is to make sure
My child knows whose birthday we are celebrating and why.

More – See Page

20___ _____ _____

20___ _____ _____

20___ _____ _____

20___ _____ _____

20___ _____ _____

20___ _____ _____

But in your hearts revere Christ as Lord.
Always be prepared to give an answer
to everyone who asks you to give the reason
for the hope that you have.
1 Peter 3:15a

December 9

I think about the perfect gifts
That I could give away. . .
Like love, some hugs, even a smile,
And more time to listen and play.

More – See Page

20____ _____ _____

_____

20____ _____ _____

_____

20____ _____ _____

_____

20____ _____ _____

_____

20____ _____ _____

_____

20____ _____ _____

_____

Therefore receive one another,
just as Christ also received us,
to the glory of God.
Romans 15:7 NKJV

December 10

My grandchildren are my gift and joy,
We read, walk, cook, and play with their toys.
But when I need to get off my feet,
Handing them back to mom is oh so sweet!

More – See Page

20___ _____ _____

20___ _____ _____

20___ _____ _____

20___ _____ _____

20___ _____ _____

20___ _____ _____

Because of the Lord's great love
we are not consumed, for his compassions never fail.
They are new every morning;
great is your faithfulness.
Lamentations 3:22,23

December 11

Though I'm busy at work
And cannot watch you play,
Thoughts of you make me smile;
I giggled out loud one day.
During my lunch break I eat,
Then often rush to the store.
Near the tiny clothes and toys
I think of you that much more.

More – See Page

20___ _____ _____

20___ _____ _____

20___ _____ _____

20___ _____ _____

20___ _____ _____

20___ _____ _____

How precious to me are your thoughts, God!
How vast is the sum of them!
Were I to count them,
they would outnumber the grains of sand—
when I awake, I am still with you.
Psalm 139:17,18

December 12

If television is on in your home does it. . .
>Teach?
>Enlighten?
>Lift spirits?
>Entertain wholesomely?
>Vitalize?
>Inspire?
>Soothe?
>Illuminate?
>Offer options?
>Nudge when Necessary?

More – See Page

20____ _____ _____

_____

20____ _____ _____

_____

20____ _____ _____

_____

20____ _____ _____

_____

20____ _____ _____

_____

20____ _____ _____

_____

So if you're serious about living
this new resurrection life with Christ, act like it.
Pursue the things over which Christ presides.
See things from His perspective.
Colossians 3:1,2b MSG

December 13

What better way to start a new school day,
Then with a prayer and kiss before they're on their way.

More – See Page

20___ _____ _____

20___ _____ _____

20___ _____ _____

20___ _____ _____

20___ _____ _____

20___ _____ _____

Commit everything you do to the Lord.
Trust him, and he will help you.
Psalm 37:5 NLT

December 14

No one spilled the milk today,
Nobody cried when they didn't get their way.
No one fought for the same toy,
Nobody got hit by the bully boy.
Now that I think of it,
I did have a great day—
By counting my blessings
In this very strange way.

More – See Page

20____

20____

20____

20____

20____

20____

Give thanks to the Lord, for he is good;
his love endures forever.
1 Chronicles 16:34

December 15

I love the funny things my children often say,
They make me smile and bring me joy most any day.
Sometimes my children repeat what their little ears think they hear
But by changing a word or two, their words become oh so dear.
Other times, I have no idea where their words originate
Giving me a sweet keepsake they each have managed to create.
My potty-trained 5-year-old shared words that made this memory book,
He explained why he "pooped" in his pants, since he saw my surprised look.
"I gambled with a 'fart' and lost!" He simply but sheepishly had to say,
We both laughed and giggled, changed his pants, then he ran off to play.

More – See Page

20___ _____ _____

20___ _____ _____

20___ _____ _____

20___ _____ _____

20___ _____ _____

20___ _____ _____

Worry weighs a person down;
an encouraging word cheers a person up.
Proverbs 12:25 NLT

December 16

Math and science are good for my child to know;
I'm sure facts and figures will help his mind grow.
But if taught alone without learning rules of the heart—
Forgiveness and love—his teaching has just been in part.

More – See Page

20____ _____ _____
_____

20____ _____ _____
_____

20____ _____ _____
_____

20____ _____ _____
_____

20____ _____ _____
_____

20____ _____ _____
_____

The fear of the Lord
is the beginning of wisdom,
and knowledge of the Holy One
is understanding.
Proverbs 9:10

December 17

How can I feel lonely –
When there are so many people around?
How can I feel lonely –
When there is never a quiet sound?
But I do feel lonely –
My heart aches from deep inside.
I need You, don't leave me. . .
Come be with me at my side.

More – See Page

20____ _____ _____

20____ _____ _____

20____ _____ _____

20____ _____ _____

20____ _____ _____

20____ _____ _____

Do not be afraid or discouraged,
for the Lord will personally go ahead of you.
He will be with you;
he will neither fail you nor abandon you.
Deuteronomy 31:8 NLT

December 18

There are so few toy stores left where I can walk down an aisle,
Looking at dolls, games, or even pushing a truck on the tile.
My children have always liked joining me to search, to see, and touch.
They'd put toys on a "wish list," or save-up when the cost was too much.
I know I could order toys on-line from my computer screen on my lap;
But we like to explore and touch instead of ordering with a keyboard tap.
I also want them to laugh, play games, learning to share with one another,
Instead of staring at a screen, not playing with a friend, sister or brother.
I know the world's changing quickly, but I'll continue to search until I find,
"Mom and Pop" stores with fun, interactive toys that are one of a kind.

More – See Page

20____ _____ _____

20____ _____ _____

20____ _____ _____

20____ _____ _____

20____ _____ _____

20____ _____ _____

Command them to do good,
to be rich in good deeds,
and to be generous and willing to share.
1 Timothy 6:18

December 19

The sparkle in my children's eyes
Of wonder, awe, and delight
Shines brighter than a Christmas light
Glowing bright into the dark night.

More – See Page

20___ _____ _____

20___ _____ _____

20___ _____ _____

20___ _____ _____

20___ _____ _____

20___ _____ _____

Your eye is a lamp that provides light for you your body.
When your eye is good, your whole body is filled with light.
If you are filled with light, with no dark corners,
then your whole life will be radiant,
as though a floodlight were filling you with light.
Luke 11:34,36 NLT

December 20

My children sing in the front row,
"Jesus loves me this I know."
The song is old, but the words are true:
Help them believe and trust in You.

More – See Page

20___ _____ _____

20___ _____ _____

20___ _____ _____

20___ _____ _____

20___ _____ _____

20___ _____ _____

Taking the child in his arms, he said to them,
"Anyone who welcomes a little child like this on my behalf
welcomes me, and anyone who welcomes me
welcomes not only me
but also my Father who sent me."
Mark 9:36b,37 NLT

December 21

Young children hear our words of love and concern
Much more readily when our eyes meet at the same level.

More – See Page

20____ _____ _____

_____

20____ _____ _____

_____

20____ _____ _____

_____

20____ _____ _____

_____

20____ _____ _____

_____

20____ _____ _____

_____

In your relationships with one another,
have the same mindset as Christ Jesus:
Who, being in very nature God, did not consider equality with God
something to be used to his own advantage;
rather, he made himself nothing
by taking the very nature of a servant,
being made in human likeness.
Philippians 2:5-7

December 22

To keep my home centered and honoring only You
I need to pray daily, asking what You want me to do.

More – See Page

20___ _____ _____

20___ _____ _____

20___ _____ _____

20___ _____ _____

20___ _____ _____

20___ _____ _____

"Ask and it will be given to you;
seek and you will find;
knock and the door will be opened to you.
For everyone who asks receives;
the one who seeks finds;
and to the one who knocks,
the door will be opened."
Matthew 7:7,8

December 23

Read me more Mommy. . .
About the first Christmas day
When Jesus was born and slept on the hay.
Read me more Mommy. . .
Did He cry? Was He cold?
Why is it the greatest story ever told?
Read me more Mommy. . .
About the three Wisemen's gifts.
Do you think He'd like my big hug and kiss?

More – See Page

20____ _____ _____

20____ _____ _____

20____ _____ _____

20____ _____ _____

20____ _____ _____

20____ _____ _____

For there is born to you this day in the city of David
a Savior, who is Christ the Lord.
And this will be the sign to you:
You will find a Babe wrapped in swaddling cloths
lying in a manger."
Luke 2:11,12 NKJV

358

December 24

No ornaments, no carols, or even snow,
In the little town of Bethlehem long ago.
No hotel, no home, no room for them at all,
Just the warmth of a manger in a lowly stall.
God gave us this gift! God gave us His Son!
Let there be peace and love for everyone.

More – See Page

20___ _____ _____

20___ _____ _____

20___ _____ _____

20___ _____ _____

20___ _____ _____

20___ _____ _____

For you know the grace of our Lord Jesus Christ,
that though he was rich, yet for your sake he became poor,
so that you through his poverty might become rich.
2 Corinthians 8:9

December 25

JESUS! TODAY'S YOUR BIRTHDAY!

We've made You a cake,
Put a candle on it too.
Before we open presents
We'll sing, "Happy Birthday to You!"

More – See Page

20____ _____ _____

_____

20____ _____ _____

_____

20____ _____ _____

_____

20____ _____ _____

_____

20____ _____ _____

_____

20____ _____ _____

_____

For unto us a Child is born, unto us a Son is given;
and the government will be upon his shoulder.
And his name will be called Wonderful, Counselor,
Mighty God, Everlasting Father, Prince of Peace.
Isaiah 9:6 NKJV

December 26

Your child is the future;
He could change this place.
He's watching and learning
From the problems you face.
He mimics what you do,
He repeats what you say;
You're the most important influence
On how he will grow each day.

. . .continued

More – See Page

20____ _____ _____

20____ _____ _____

20____ _____ _____

20____ _____ _____

20____ _____ _____

20____ _____ _____

If you are wise and understand God's ways,
prove it by living an honorable life,
doing good works with the humility
that comes from wisdom.
James 3:13 NLT

December 27

It's an awesome responsibility,
But you don't have to feel alone.
There's a source of strength and direction
To use as your cornerstone.
It's very simple to receive
And doesn't take much time.
Just mean it from your heart
And it's yours for a lifetime.

. . .continued

More – See Page

20___ _____ _____

20___ _____ _____

20___ _____ _____

20___ _____ _____

20___ _____ _____

20___ _____ _____

But God demonstrates his own love for us in this:
While we were still sinners, Christ died for us.
Romans 5:8

December 28

Say, "Lord, I need Your help
To raise Your precious gift.
I cannot do it alone,
I need Your spiritual lift.
Lord, please take control
Of the good days and the bad;
Please forgive my many sins!
I give to You the power I thought I had.

. . .continued

More – See Page

20___ _____ _____

20___ _____ _____

20___ _____ _____

20___ _____ _____

20___ _____ _____

20___ _____ _____

If you confess with your mouth that Jesus is Lord
and believe in your heart that God raised him from the dead,
you will be saved.
For everyone who calls on the name of the Lord will be saved.
Romans 10:9,13 NLT

December 29

"I thank You, too, Lord,
For dying in my place for my sin.
I receive You as my Savior.
Please, Lord, do come in!
Make me the daughter,
Wife, and mother, You have in mind.
You're in control now,
You're the *source* I've needed to find."

. . .continued

More – See Page

20____ _____ _____

20____ _____ _____

20____ _____ _____

20____ _____ _____

20____ _____ _____

20____ _____ _____

For the wages of sin is death,
but the gift of God is eternal life in Christ Jesus our Lord.
Romans 6:23

Therefore, if anyone is in Christ, the new creation has come:
The old has gone, the new is here!
2 Corinthians 5:17

December 30

By praying this today,
Be assured, He's in your life.
Helping you each moment,
Especially those filled with strife.
So use Him, rely on Him,
Talk to Him every day.
Thank Him, cry to Him,
He'll show you the way.

. . .continued

More – See Page

20___ _____ _____

20___ _____ _____

20___ _____ _____

20___ _____ _____

20___ _____ _____

20___ _____ _____

So then, just as you received Christ Jesus as Lord,
continue to live your lives in him, rooted and built up in him,
strengthened in the faith as you were taught,
and overflowing with thankfulness.
Colossians 2:6,7

December 31

He'll make you confident in your decisions.
He will always be right there by your side.
He will give you love, patience, and wisdom.
You've now found the source, so let Him guide!

More – See Page

20___ _____ _____

_____

20___ _____ _____

_____

20___ _____ _____

_____

20___ _____ _____

_____

20___ _____ _____

_____

20___ _____ _____

_____

Christ Jesus died for us and was raised to life for us,
and he is sitting in the place of honor at God's right hand,
pleading for us.
No power in the sky above or in the earth below—
indeed, nothing in all creation will ever be able to separate us
from the love of God that is revealed in Christ Jesus our Lord.
Romans 8:34,39 NLT

Bible Verse Index

OLD TESTAMENT

139:23,24 NLT – 10/22; **141:3** – 6/23; **145:4,5** NLT – 10/6; **146:1,2** – 3/5; **147:3** – 5/5; **147:3** NLT – 9/2

PROVERBS - **1:5,7** – 10/20; **1:8** – 3/17; **1:10** NLT – 11/2; **1:33** – 11/5; **2:6** – 9/25; **2:10,11** NLT – 8/26; **3:3** – 9/17; **3:5,6** NLT – 3/14; **3:11,12** NLT – 10/18; **3:13,14,17,18** – 10/1; **4:3,4** – 11/30; **6:20** – 11/6; **8:32,33,34** – 7/1; **9:8b,9** NLT – 4/17; **9:10** – 12/16; **10:1a** – 9/12; **10:12b** NLT – 8/16; **12:1** NLT – 3/4; **12:15** NLT -7/23; **12:19** NLT – 8/13; **12:22** – 4/8; **12:22** NLT – 11/4; **12:25** NLT – 12/15; **13:19a** – 8/1; **14:29** – 6/14; **14:30** NLT – 5/4; **15:1** -10/30; **15:13** -1/28; **15:15b** MSG – 3/24; **15:15** NLT – 8/30; **15:30** NLT – 3/1; **15:32** NLT – 7/17; **16:9** NLT – 10/24; **16:21** NLT – 7/25; **16:23** NLT – 9/14; **16:24** NLT – 2/16; **16:31** NLT – 9/1; **17:17** – 6/18; **17:22** NLT – 9/9; **18:10** NKJ – 8/10; **19:11** – 5/8; **19:21** NLT – 12/2; **19:27** – 1/19; **20:11** – 10/16; **22:6** NKJV – 2/17; **22:6** – 4/6; **22:6** NLT – 11/1; **23:12** NLT – 8/2; **23:15,16** NLT – 8/14; **23:22,24,25** NLT – 10/9; **24:3** NLT – 11/16; **24:16a** NLT 0 9/5; **27:9b** MSG – 3/28; **29:11** – 3/12; **29:17** MSG – 1/14; **29:17** – 6/20; **31:10** – 5/19; **31:15,19** MSG– 2/5; **31:20** – 2/24; **31:26** – 10/29; **31:27,28** – 6/5; **31:30** NLT – 1/13

ECCLESIASTES - **3:1** – 11/20; **3:1,4** – 4/14; **3:1,7** – 5/21; **3:1,12,13** NKJV – 9/10; **3:11** – 10/26; **4:9,10,12a** NLT – 5/29; **7:8** – 7/15; **8:5b** NLT – 6/7; **8:5b,6** NLT – 11/5

ISAIAH - **9:6** NKJV – 12/25; **40:8** – 5/11; **40:11** – 11/25; **40:28,29** – 11/17; **40:11** -6/27; **40:30,31** – 4/3; **41:10** NLT – 1/30; **43:18,19** NLT – 12/1; **44:8b** – 8/17; **54:13** – 5/2; **64:8** – 6/10

JEREMIAH - **29:11,12,13** – 4/16; **31:3** – 3/21; **31:25** – 5/22

LAMENTATIONS - **2:19** NLT – 7/31; **3:22,23** – 12/10

DANIEL - **10:12** NLTL – 1/15

MICAH - **6:8** NKJV – 3/31

ZEPHANNIAH - **3:17** NKJV – 12/6

ZACHARIAH - **7:9** – 10/23

MALACHI - **3:8,10** NLT– 9/15

NEW TESTAMENT

MATTHEW - **5:1,2,4** – 9/11; **5:5** – 4/26; **5:16** NLT – 10/13; **5:23,24** – 9/29; **5:43,44,45a** NLT – 7/12; **6:3,4** MSG – 7/19; **6:9,10,11,12,13** NKJV – 4/5; **6:19-21** – 1/2; **6:24** – 11/3; **6:25,27** – 2/28; **6:33** – 6/16; **6:30** MSG – 2/1; **6:34** MSG – 7/24; **7:1,2** – 5/14; **7:7-8** – 12/22; **7:12** NLT – 11/4; **7:13,14** – 6/30; **7:24,26,27** – 7/11; **9:20,21,22** – 2/22; **11:28** NLT – 5/16; **11:28** – 8/7; **12: 34b,35a** NLT – 8/19; **12:48,49,50** – 3/18; **18:3,4,5** – 11/24; **19:14** – 4/25; **22:37,38,39,40** NLT – 11/11; **24:42,43,44** – 10/8; **25:40** – 12/4; **28:20** NLT– 3/11

MARK - **4:18,19** – 6/9; **6:41a42,43,44** – 8/31; **9:36b,37** NLT– 12/20; **10:45** – 9/30; **12: 29,30,31** NLT – 12/5

LUKE - **1;39,40,41,44,45** NLT – 7/9; **2:11,12** NKJV – 12/23; **5:5,6** – 5/24; **5:13** – 8/24; **6:37** – 8/15; **6:41,42** – 7/14; **8:16,17** – 10/10; **10:38,39,41,42** NLT – 6/11; **11:34,36** NLT – 12/19; **12:27** – 5/1

JOHN - **1:16** NLT – 11/15; **8:34,35,36** – 7/4; **13:34,35** NLT – 1/18; **13:34,35** MSG – 8/27; **14:6,7,11** NLT – 9/24; **14:6,12,13** NLT – 1/8; **14:21** – 1/22; **15:12** – 1/25; **15:13** NLT – 5/30; **15:14,15** – 8/5

ROMANS - **5:3,4** – 3/3; **5:8** – 12/27; **5:8** – 5/26; **6:23** – 12/29; **8:34,39** NLT – 12/31; **8:38a** NLT – 7/3; **10:9,13** NLT – 12/28; **12:1** – 5/27; **12:10** – 8/3; **12:10,13** – 3/25, **12:12** NLT – 5/17; **12:15** – 5/20; **15:2,3** MSG – 8/20; **15:5** – 11/22; **15:7** NKJV – 12/9

1 CORINTHIANS - **10:12** – 4/1; **11:1** – 6/4; **13:4a** – 6/29; **13:1-7** – 2/9-13; **13:7** NLT– 4/27; **13:11** NKJV - 11/2; **15:33** – 4/2

2 CORINTHIANS - **1:4** NLT – 9/27; **2:14b,15a** NLT – 11/8; **5:17**- 12/29; **6:4a,6** NLT – 12/7; **8:7** – 4/28; **8:9** – 12/24; **9:6** – 6/21; **9:7,8** – 10/17; **10:5b** – 6/25; **12:9** – 5/28

GALATIANS - **6:2**-4/12; **6:9** - 3/16; **6:9** NLT – 4/22

EPHESIANS - **2:8,9,10** NLT – 7/18; **2:10** – 7/6; **4:1b,2** – 1/23; **4:1,2**, NLT – 9/21; **4:1,2** – 10/7; **4:25,26a** – 7/13; **4:26,27** NLT – 2/8; **4:29** NLT – 6/6;

4:32 NLT – 1/3; **5:15,16,17** NLT – 6/3; **5:19b,20** – 3/29; **5:19,20** MSG – 7/22; **5:31** NLT – 1/12; **5:31,32,33** NLT – 2/14; **6:1-3** – 11/1; **6:1-3** MSG – 1/9; **6:4** – 2/21

PHILIPPIANS - 1:6 MSG – 9/13; **2:3,4** NLT – 8/9; **2:2,3,4** NLT- 1/24; **2:2,3,4,5** NKJV – 9/3; **2:5,6,7** – 12/21; **4:4** – 1/1; **4:6,7** MSG – 9/18; **4:6,7** – 2/19; **4:8** – 3/26; **4:9** NLT -9/19; **4:12b,13** – 2/20; **4:12b,13** – 8/22; **4:19** – 1/10; **4:19** NLT – 5/23;

COLOSSIANS - 1:11 NLT – 2/26; **1:11** – 8/6; **1:15,16a** NLT – 9/23; **2:6,7** – 12/30; **3:1,2** MSG – 12/12; **3:12** – 1/6; **3:13** – 11/27; **3:13,14** – 6/17; **3:15**- 11/12; **3:16** NLT- 10/3; **3:17** NLT- 7/27; **3:23** – 7/20; **4:2** – 3/23; **4:2,6** NLT – 8/18

1 THESSALONIANS - 3:12 – 9/6; **5:11** – 3/30; **5:14b** NLT – 9/20; **5:16,17,18** NLT – 4/7; **5:18** – 8/4; **5:25** NLT – 9/16;

2 THESSALONIANS - 3:3 – 3/27

1 TIMOTHY - 4:12 – 11/19; **4:15** MSG – 5/13; **6:18** – 12/18

2 TIMOTHY - 2:22 NLT – 6/8; **3:15** NLT – 11/14; **3:15** NLT – 5/18; **3:16,17** NLT – 8/23

TITUS - 1:6A,9 NLT – 4/11; **3:1** NLT – 11/3

HEBREWS - 3:13 – 2/23; **4:9,10** – 6/28; **10:22a** NLT – 5/7; **10:24** NLT – 9/22; **11:1** NLT – 4/30; **12:11** – 10/14; **13:5b,6a** – 8/21; **13:16** – 12/3

JAMES - 1:5,6 -8/25; **1:17** – 1/11; **1:19** – 7/10; **2:1** – 4/10; **2:1,9** NLT – 1/20; **3:2** NLT – 3/19; **3:3,4,5** MSG - 4/29; **3:13** NLT – 12/26; **3:17** NKJV – 6/27; **4:17** NLT – 2/15;

1 PETER - 3:8,9,10,11,12 MSG – 7/26; **3:15a** – 12/8; **4:8** – 1/29; **4:8** NLT – 10/12; **4:8,9** NLT – 7/8; **5:7** – 7/6

1 JOHN - 2:1,2 – 10/15; **3:1** – 4/15; **3:18** – 4/19; **4:9,10,19** – 10/2; **4:12** – 7/5

3 JOHN - 1:4 – 5/9

More Milestones, Memories & Moments

Date   Continued Memory

More Milestones, Memories & Moments

Date · Continued Memory

_____ ·

More Milestones, Memories & Moments

Date	Continued Memory

More Milestones, Memories & Moments

Date   Continued Memory

_____   _____

               _____

               _____

               _____

               _____

               _____

_____   _____

               _____

               _____

               _____

               _____

               _____

_____   _____

               _____

               _____

               _____

               _____

               _____

_____   _____

               _____

               _____

               _____

               _____

               _____

_____   _____

               _____

               _____

               _____

               _____

More Milestones, Memories & Moments

Date   Continued Memory

_____   _____

       _____

       _____

       _____

       _____

_____   _____

       _____

       _____

       _____

       _____

_____   _____

       _____

       _____

       _____

       _____

_____   _____

       _____

       _____

       _____

       _____

_____   _____

       _____

       _____

       _____

More Milestones, Memories & Moments

Date   **Continued Memory**

More Milestones, Memories & Moments

Date   Continued Memory

_____   _____

           _____

           _____

           _____

           _____

_____   _____

           _____

           _____

           _____

           _____

_____   _____

           _____

           _____

           _____

           _____

_____   _____

           _____

           _____

           _____

           _____

_____   _____

           _____

           _____

           _____

           _____

More Milestones, Memories & Moments

Date   Continued Memory

More Milestones, Memories & Moments

Date   Continued Memory

_____   _____

           _____

           _____

           _____

           _____

           _____

_____   _____

           _____

           _____

           _____

           _____

           _____

_____   _____

           _____

           _____

           _____

           _____

           _____

_____   _____

           _____

           _____

           _____

           _____

           _____

_____   _____

           _____

           _____

           _____

           _____

           _____

More Milestones, Memories & Moments

Date   Continued Memory

_____   _____

                _____

                _____

                _____

                _____

                _____

_____   _____

                _____

                _____

                _____

                _____

                _____

_____   _____

                _____

                _____

                _____

                _____

_____   _____

                _____

                _____

                _____

                _____

_____   _____

                _____

                _____

                _____

                _____

More Milestones, Memories & Moments

Date   **Continued Memory**

_____   _____

            _____

            _____

            _____

            _____

            _____

_____   _____

            _____

            _____

            _____

            _____

_____   _____

            _____

            _____

            _____

            _____

_____   _____

            _____

            _____

            _____

            _____

_____   _____

            _____

            _____

            _____

More Milestones, Memories & Moments

Date   **Continued Memory**

_____   _____

             _____

             _____

             _____

             _____

             _____

_____   _____

             _____

             _____

             _____

             _____

_____   _____

             _____

             _____

             _____

             _____

_____   _____

             _____

             _____

             _____

             _____

_____   _____

             _____

             _____

             _____

             _____

More Milestones, Memories & Moments

Date   Continued Memory

_____   _____
               _____
               _____
               _____
               _____
_____   _____
               _____
               _____
               _____
               _____
_____   _____
               _____
               _____
               _____
               _____
_____   _____
               _____
               _____
               _____
               _____
_____   _____
               _____
               _____
               _____
               _____

More Milestones, Memories & Moments

Date   Continued Memory

More Milestones, Memories & Moments

Date   Continued Memory

_____

_____

_____

_____

_____

More Milestones, Memories & Moments

Date	Continued Memory

More Milestones, Memories & Moments

Date	Continued Memory
————	_____
	_____
	_____
	_____
	_____
	_____
————	_____
	_____
	_____
	_____
	_____
————	_____
	_____
	_____
	_____
	_____
————	_____
	_____
	_____
	_____
	_____
————	_____
	_____
	_____
	_____

More Milestones, Memories & Moments

Date	Continued Memory
_____	_____
	_____
	_____
	_____
	_____
_____	_____
	_____
	_____
	_____
	_____
_____	_____
	_____
	_____
	_____
_____	_____
	_____
	_____
	_____
	_____
_____	_____
	_____
	_____
	_____

More Milestones, Memories & Moments

Date	Continued Memory

With Heartfelt Thanks

This book and the original **Mother's Moments** is because of and dedicated to my Lord and Savior, Jesus Christ. He has **shown** Himself to me in so many miraculous ways. Poems poured effortlessly out of my pen. Sometimes I could barely keep up with the flowing creative thoughts. Because of His divine appointment in 1990, I want to thank the very talented illustrator, Priscilla Burris, who suggested I write, and then she would illustrate, the 366 pages of the original calendar. That is where it all began.

I also want to thank from my heart:

My **husband,** Ken, for his love, support, prayers, delicious meals, and being my detail-oriented Managing Editor.

My **adult children**: Cambria-who made me a grandma, was my inspiration for many of these new poems and helped me stay on track for reaching today's moms; for Scott, our Aerospace Engineer, who had amazing insight and specific suggestions; and for Danielle, our Masters in Counseling graduate, who was there to encourage and edit.

My **dear friends** who knew the Bible better than me and helped me find many of the coordinating Bible verses on each page: Mardel Yeates, Dawn Curtis, Amy Palace, Lisa Johnson and Jan, Kira and Abby Waite – Also thanks to Kelly Hansen for her encouragement and her creative computer skills.

My **amazing editor** and friend, Julia Weber, who meticulously reviewed and edited every aspect of this Keepsake Memory Journal.

My **many friends** across the country who took time to read and evaluate my new and revised poems.

The **publishers and gifted writers** of two daily devotionals who inspire me daily in many ways: **"In Touch"** magazine from *In Touch Ministries* in Atlanta, Georgia, and **"Our Daily Bread"** from *Our Daily Bread Ministries* in Grand Rapids, MI.

My **many young mom friends** through *MOPS* (Mothers Of Pre-Schoolers), my neighbors, friends at church, *Bible Study Fellowship,* and moms I meet through *Love In the Name of Christ.* They have welcomed me into their lives and have shared their joys, tears, questions, and challenges of raising children. It has inspired and reminded me that God has called and equipped me to reach out and encourage moms with young children. It is my love and passion.

To all I thank you for being part of this exciting journey in creating:
Mom's Moment's ~ Smiles to Remember.

Whoever has my commands and obeys them, he is the one who loves me. He who loves me will be loved by my Father, and I too will love him and SHOW myself to him.
John 14:21 NIV

CPSIA information can be obtained
at www.ICGtesting.com
Printed in the USA
LVHW052136110419
613853LV00002B/2/P

9 781545 662496